P9-DGQ-355

POPULAR CULTURE IN AMERICA
1800-1925

POPULAR CULTURE IN AMERICA

1800-1925

MAKING HIS WAY

OR

FRANK COURTNEY'S STRUGGLE UPWARD

BY

HORATIO ALGER JR.

ARNO PRESS
A New York Times Company
New York • 1974

Reprint Edition 1974 by Arno Press Inc.

POPULAR CULTURE IN AMERICA: 1800-1925
ISBN for complete set: 0-405-06360-1
See last pages of this volume for titles.

Publisher's Note: This book was reprinted from the best available copy.

Manufactured in the United States of America

Library of Congress Cataloging in Publication Data

Alger, Horatio, 1832-1899.
Making his way.

(Popular culture in America)
Reprint of the ed. published by Hurst, New York, in the Alger series for boys.
SUMMARY: Young Frank Courtney's perseverance, ambition, and high moral character ultimately enable him to triump.
I. Title. II. Series.
PZ7.A395Mak12 [Fic] 74-15724
ISBN 0-405-06361-X

MAKING HIS WAY

OR

FRANK COURTNEY'S STRUGGLE UPWARD

BY

HORATIO ALGER JR.

AUTHOR OF "ONLY AN IRISH BOY," "STRIVE AND SUCCEED," "DO AND DARE," "FACING THE WORLD," "IN A NEW WORLD," "BOB BURTON."

NEW YORK
HURST & COMPANY
PUBLISHERS

MAKING HIS WAY.

CHAPTER I.

TWO SCHOOL FRIENDS.

Two boys were walking in the campus of the Bridgeville Academy. They were apparently of about the same age—somewhere from fifteen to sixteen—but there was a considerable difference in their attire.

Herbert Grant was neatly but coarsely dressed, and his shoes were of cowhide, but his face indicated a frank, sincere nature, and was expressive of intelligence.

His companion was dressed in a suit of fine cloth, his linen was of the finest, his shoes were of calfskin, and he had the indefinable air of a boy who had been reared in luxury.

He had not the broad, open face of his friend—for the two boys were close friends—but his features were finely chiseled, indicating a share of pride, and a bold, self-reliant nature.

He, too, was an attractive boy, and in spite of his pride possessed a warm, affectionate heart and sterling qualities, likely to endear him to those who could read and understand him.

His name was Frank Courtney, and he is the hero of my story.

"Have you written your Latin exercises, Frank?" asked Herbert.

"Yes; I finished them an hour ago."

"I was going to ask you to write them with me. It is pleasanter to study in company."

"Provided you have the right sort of company," rejoined Frank.

"Am I the right sort of company?" inquired Herbert, with a smile.

"You hardly need to ask that, Herbert. Are we not always together? If I did not like your company, I should not seek it so persistently. I don't care to boast, but I have plenty of offers of companionship which I don't care to accept. There is Bob Stickney, for instance, who is always inviting me to his room; but you know what he is—a lazy fellow, who cares more to have a good time than to study. Then there is James Cameron, a conceited, empty-headed fellow, who is very disagreeable to me."

"You don't mention your stepbrother, Mark Manning."

"For two reasons—he doesn't care for my company, and of all the boys I dislike him the most."

"I don't like him myself. But why do you dislike him so much?"

"Because he is a sneak—a crafty, deceitful fellow, always scheming for his own interest. He hates me, but he doesn't dare to show it.

His father is my mother's husband, but the property is hers, and will be mine. He thinks he may some day be dependent on me, and he conceals his dislike in order to stand the better chance by and by. Heaven grant that it may be long before my dear mother is called away!"

"How did she happen to marry again, Frank?"

"I can hardly tell. It was a great grief to me. Mr. Manning was a penniless lawyer, who ingratiated himself with my mother, and persecuted her till she consented to marry him. He is very soft-spoken, and very plausible, and he managed to make mother—who has been an invalid for years—think that it would be the best thing for her to delegate her cares to him, and provide me with a second father."

There was a scornful bitterness in Frank's tones as he pronounced these last words.

"Well," he continued, "he had managed to extract a promise from mother, before I knew or suspected his design. It was three years since, and I was not quite thirteen; but I can well remember how badly I felt when mother told me of the engagement. I remonstrated strongly, till I saw that she was becoming nervous and agitated, and only desisted because I did not want to pain her. I tried hard to treat Mr. Manning civilly, but I have no doubt I seemed cold and sulky. At any rate, the marriage took place, and Mr. Manning and

Mark came to the Cedars to live. You know that is the name of our place."

"Yes. It must have been very disagreeable to you."

"I can hardly tell you how much so."

"How has your stepfather treated you?"

"I am bound to say, Herbert, that I have nothing to complain of. He has not attempted to control or tyrannize over me. He has always been polite, and has tried to be fatherly. If anything, I should say that he has been too deferential and too soft-spoken. I have not had any of my privileges curtailed, or been deprived of anything to which I was accustomed."

"I am surprised at that. That is not the general reputation of stepfathers."

"That is true, Herbert; but I am convinced that Mr. Manning is not acting himself. He has an object in disguising his real nature. He is my secret enemy—I am sure of that—and some time or other he will show himself in his true colors. That will not probably affect me while my dear mother lives. The property is hers, and he would lose his hold upon her and the management of the estate if he should ill-treat me. I heartily hope that mother will live till I am a man. I shall then feel better able to defeat my stepfather's schemes."

"Your mother is likely to live, is she not, Frank?"

"She is in a consumption, Herbert," said Frank, gravely. "It is in her family. Still, there may be no immediate danger. Her oldest sister, my Aunt Maria, lived for twenty years after her lungs had become affected, and this gives me hope that mother may linger as long."

"Mr. Manning is kind to her, I hope?"

Frank's eyes flashed.

"He would not dare be anything else!" he answered, quickly. "This is all that reconciles me to the marriage," he went on, more calmly. "My stepfather is certainly attentive and kind to my mother. His soft manner seems to me sometimes rather sickening and unmanly. Still, mother's nature is gentle, and if it suits her, I have nothing to say."

"Your stepbrother, Mark Manning, enjoys the same advantages as yourself, does he not?" inquired Herbert.

"Yes."

"Then his father's marriage proved a good thing for him."

"That is true. When he first came to the house he was poorly dressed, and had evidently been used to living in a poor way. He was at once provided with a complete outfit as good as my own, and from that time as much has been spent on him as on me. Don't think that I am mean enough to grudge him any part of the money expended upon him. If he were like you, I could like him, and enjoy his society; but he is just such another as his father."

"That reminds me, Frank, to ask you a question. How is it that you, who are rich, and the heir of a large fortune, have become the friend of a poor boy like me? I am the son of a poor carpenter, who has hard work to provide a decent living for his family, yet you take more notice of me than of any other boy in the academy."

"Take notice isn't the right way to express yourself, Herbert. That would imply inferiority on your part."

"Most people would consider me inferior, Frank."

"Just because I am richer than you? I am not so foolish. If I were to lose all my money, would you like me any less?"

"Not a bit, Frank."

"Then you see money has nothing to do with it. I go with you, Herbert, because I like you. You don't want me to flatter you, and so I won't explain why I like you. I should like nothing better than to have you with me for the next few years."

"That can't be," said Herbert, sighing. "You will go to college, but there is no chance of that for me."

"I have been thinking of that, Herbert," said Frank, earnestly, "but I didn't like to tell you what I proposed until I knew whether I could carry it out. I am going to ask my mother to pay your expenses through college. You could room with me, and I would promise to be extra economical, if necessary, in order to make the additional expense less."

Herbert was surprised and moved by this generous proposal. He put his arm affectionately round the neck of his friend, and said, impulsively:

"Dear Frank, how kind you are! But it would be altogether too much for you to give or me to accept."

"No, it wouldn't, Herbert. Do you think I would value the money in comparison with the pleasure I should have in your society, and the satisfaction of feeling that I was helping you on in the world? When you became a great lawyer or statesman, I should take credit to myself for having given you the chance to become distinguished."

"I might disappoint you, Frank. You would be more likely to become distinguished than I."

"There would be no rivalry between us, but we would try to improve our advantages."

"It may never come to pass, Frank, but I will not forget your kind intentions. I should like nothing better than to go to college, now that I am so nearly prepared. Some people think father foolish not to have taken me from the academy sooner, but he says a good education will always help me. Even without going to college, I know enough to teach a common school, and when I am old enough I shall probably become a teacher."

"Provided I cannot arrange better for you."

Here Herbert's attention was drawn to a boy who was approaching with a yellow envelope in his hand.

"Frank," he said, suddenly, "there's Mark Manning. He looks as if he had something to say to you. He has either a letter or a telegram in his hand."

CHAPTER II.

THE TELEGRAM.

FRANK'S heart gave a great bound at the suggestion of a telegram. A telegram could mean but one thing—that his mother had become suddenly worse.

He hurried to meet his stepbrother.

"Is that a telegram, Mark?" he asked, anxiously.

"Yes."

"Is it anything about mother? Tell me quick!"

"Read it for yourself, Frank."

Frank drew the telegram from the envelope, and read it hastily:

"My wife is very sick. I wish you and Frank to come home at once."

"When does the next train start, Herbert?" asked Frank, pale with apprehension.

"In an hour."

"I shall go by that train."

"I don't think I can get ready so soon," said Mark, deliberately.

"Then you can come by yourself," replied Frank, impetuously. "I beg your pardon, Mark," he added. "I cannot expect you to feel as I do. It is not your mother."

"It is my stepmother," said Mark.

"That is quite different. But I must not linger here. I will go at once to Dr. Brush, and tell him of my summons home. Good-by, Herbert, till we meet again."

"I will go with you to the depot, Frank," said his friend, sympathizingly. "Don't wait for me. Go ahead, and make your preparation for the journey. I will be at your room in a quarter of an hour."

"You won't go by the next train, Mark?" said Herbert.

"No. I don't care to rush about as Frank is doing."

"You would if it were your own mother who was so ill."

"I am not sure. It wouldn't do any good, would it?"

"You would naturally feel anxious," said Herbert.

"Oh, yes, I suppose so!" answered Mark, indifferently.

Mark Manning was slender and dark, with a soft voice and rather effeminate ways. He didn't care for the rough sports in which most boys delight; never played baseball or took part in athletic exercises, but liked to walk about, sprucely dressed, and had even been seen on the campus on a Saturday afternoon with his hands incased in kid gloves.

For this, however, he was so ridiculed and laughed at that he had to draw them off and replace them in his pocket.

It is needless to say that he was not a favorite among his schoolfellows.

At a large school, manliness commands respect and favor, and an effeminate boy, unless caused by ill-health, is ridiculed or despised.

For this, however, Mark cared little. He, as well as Frank, was liberally supplied with spending money, and was content to follow his own course, whether it suited his schoolfellows or not.

The Cedars, the handsome residence of Frank's family, was situated about twenty miles from Bridgeville, the seat of the classical academy at which the stepbrothers were being educated.

It was the custom of both to go home on Saturday morning, and return by an early train on Monday.

It was now the middle of the week, and, therefore, nearly three days had passed since Frank had seen his mother. Then, though weak, she had not seemed more so than usual, and he had come away from home feeling no particular anxiety.

It was evident that his mother's disease had taken a sudden and unfavorable turn.

As Frank and Herbert walked together to the railway station, the latter said:

"It seems to me, Frank, that the telegram should have been sent to you, rather than to Mark Manning. You are the one who is most interested in the contents."

"I thought of that, Herbert, but I was too much affected by the contents to speak of it. I am not surprised, however. It is like Mr. Manning. It jarred upon me to have him speak of mother as his wife. She is so, but I never could reconcile myself to the fact."

"Do you remember your father—your own father, Frank?"

"You need not have said 'your own father.' I don't recognize Mr. Manning as a father, at all. Yes, I remember him. I was eight years old when he died. He was a fine-looking man, always kind—a man to be loved and respected. There was not a particle of similarity between him and Mr. Manning. He was strong and manly."

"How did it happen that he died so young?"

"He was the victim of a railway accident. He had gone to New York on business, and was expected back on a certain day. The train on which he was a passenger collided with a freight train, and my poor father was among the passengers who were killed. The news was almost too much for my poor mother, although she had not yet become an invalid. It brought on a fit of sickness lasting for three months. She has never been altogether well since."

"After all, Frank, the gifts of fortune, or rather Providence, are not so unequally distributed as at first appears. You are rich, but fatherless. I am poor enough, but my father and mother are both spared to me."

"I would gladly accept poverty if my father could be restored to life, and my mother be spared to me for twenty years to come."

"I am sure you would, Frank," said Herbert. "Money is valuable, but there are some things far more so."

They had reached the station by this time, and it was nearly the time for the train to start. Frank bought his ticket, and the two friends shook hands and bade each other goodby.

In an hour Frank was walking up the long avenue leading to the front door of the mansion.

The door was opened by his stepfather.

"How is mother?" asked Frank, anxiously.

"I am grieved to say that she is very sick," said Mr. Manning, in a soft voice. "She had a copious hemorrhage this morning, which has weakened her very much."

"Is she in danger?" asked Frank, anxiously.

"I fear she is," said Mr. Manning.

"I suppose I can see her?"

"Yes; but it will be better not to make her talk much."

"I will be careful, sir."

Frank waited no longer, but hurried to his mother's chamber. As he entered, and his glance fell on the bed and its occupant, he was shocked by the pale and ghastly appearance of the mother whom he so dearly loved. The thought came to him at once:

"She cannot live."

He found it difficult to repress a rising sob, but he did so for his mother's sake. He thought that it might affect her injuriously if he should display emotion.

His mother smiled faintly as he approached the bed.

"Mother," said Frank, kneeling by the bedside, "are you very weak?"

"Yes, Frank," she answered, almost in a whisper. "I think I am going to leave you."

"Oh, don't say that, mother!" burst forth in anguish from Frank's lips. "Try to live for my sake."

"I should like to live, my dear boy," whispered his mother; "but if it is God's will that I should die, I must be reconciled. I leave you in his care."

Here Mr. Manning entered the room.

"You will be kind to my boy?" said the dying mother.

"Can you doubt it, my dear?" replied her husband, in the soft tones Frank so much disliked. "I will care for him as if he were my own."

"Thank you. Then I shall die easy."

"Don't speak any more, mother. It will tire you, and perhaps bring on another hemorrhage."

"Frank is right, my dear. You had better not exert yourself any more at present."

"Didn't Mark come with you?" asked Mr. Manning of Frank.

"No, sir."

"I am surprised that he should not have done so. I sent for him as well as you."

"I believe he is coming by the next train," said Frank, indifferently. "He thought he could not get ready in time for my train."

"He should not have left you to come at such a time."

"I didn't wish him to inconvenience himself, Mr. Manning. It it had been his mother, it would have been different.

Mr. Manning did not reply. He understood very well that there was no love lost between Mark and his stepson.

CHAPTER III.

FRANK'S BEREAVEMENT.

Early in the evening Mark made his appearance. Supper had been over for an hour, and everything was cold. In a house where there is sickness, the regular course of things is necessarily interrupted, and, because he could not have his wants attended to immediately, Mark saw fit to grumble and scold the servants. He was not a favorite with them, and they did not choose to be bullied.

Deborah, who had been in the house for ten years, and so assumed the independence of an old servant, sharply reprimanded the spoiled boy.

"You ought to be ashamed, Mr. Mark," she said, "of making such a fuss when my poor mistress lies upstairs at the point of death."

"Do you know who you are talking to?" demanded Mark, imperiously, for he could, when speaking with those whom he regarded as inferiors, exchange his soft tones for a voice of authority.

"I ought to know by this time," answered Deborah, contemptuously. "There is no other in the house like you, I am glad to say."

"You are very impertinent. You forget that you are nothing but a servant."

"A servant has the right to be decently treated, Mr. Mark."

"If you don't look out," said Mark, in a blustering tone, "I will report you to my father, and have you kicked out of the house."

Deborah was naturally incensed at this rude speech, but she was spared the trouble of replying. Frank entered the room at this moment in time to hear Mark's last speech.

"What is this about being kicked out of the house?" he asked, looking from Mark to Deborah, in a tone of unconscious authority, which displeased his stepbrother.

"That is my business," replied Mark, shortly.

"Mr. Mark has threatened to have me kicked out of the house because he has to wait for his supper," said Deborah.

"It wasn't for that. It was because you were impertinent. All the same, I think it is shameful that I can't get anything to eat."

"I regret, Mark," said Frank, with cool sarcasm, "that you should be inconvenienced about your meals. Perhaps you will excuse it, as my poor mother is so sick that she requires extra attention from the servants. Deborah, if possible, don't let Mark wait much longer. It seems to be very important that he should have his supper."

"He shall have it," assured Deborah, rather enjoying the way in which Mark was put down; "that is, if he don't get me kicked out of the house."

"You had better not make any such threats in future, Mark," said Frank, significantly.

"Who's to hinder?" blustered Mark.

"I am," answered Frank, pointedly.

"You are nothing but a boy like me," retorted Mark.

"My mother is mistress here, and I represent her."

"Things may change soon," muttered Mark; but Frank had left the room and did not hear him.

Mark did not trouble himself even to inquire for his stepmother, but went out to the stable and lounged about until bedtime. He seemed very much bored, and so expressed himself.

"It's a nuisance having sickness in the house," said he, to the coachman.

"Especially if you happen to be sick yourself," said the coachman, dryly.

"It's a nuisance, anyway. A fellow can't do anything, and the house is turned upside down."

He spoke in an aggrieved tone, as if Mrs. Manning were very inconsiderate to fall sick and occasion annoyance to him.

Mark was not a favorite with the coachman, who was devoted to Frank. Like Deborah, he had been in the family before Mr. Manning gained a footing there, and was disposed to regard him and his son as interlopers, though he treated them with formal respect.

"I don't think you will be troubled long, Mr. Mark," said he, gravely.

"You mean that my stepmother will die?" inquired Mark, interested, but not appearing very much grieved.

"My poor mistress is in her last sickness, Mr. Mark."

"Oh, well, we must all die sometime!" said Mark, lightly.

"He hasn't any more heart than a grindstone," said the coachman to himself, as Mark went back to the house. "I do hope Mrs. Manning will tie up the property so that this boy and his father can't make ducks and drakes of it. It'll be bad times for us when we lose our good mistress. Old Manning's a sneak, and the boy's a little worse, if anything. Frank's a fine, manly boy, and worth a dozen of him."

Frank wished to sit up all night with his mother, but, as she had a professional nurse, it was thought best that he should obtain his regular rest, the nurse promising to call the family if any change should be apparent in her patient's condition.

About half-past four in the morning there was a summons.

"Mrs. Manning is worse," said the nurse. "I don't think she can last long."

Mr. Manning and Frank hastened into the death chamber. Mark protested that he was too tired to get up, and, in spite of his father's remonstrance, remained in bed. Frank was too absorbed in his own sorrow to notice or care for Mark's absence.

If he had thought about it at all, he would have considered it a relief that his stepbrother should be away. His mother was lying in a stupor, but recovered for a few minutes before death.

One last glance of love—though she could no longer speak—assured Frank that she knew him and loved him to the last.

The memory of that look often came back to him in the years that followed, and he would not have parted with it for anything that earth could give.

Just as the clock struck five, his mother breathed her last. The boy gazed upon the inanimate form, but he was dazed, and could not realize that his mother had left him, never to return.

"She is gone," said Mr. Manning, softly.

"Dead!" ejaculated Frank.

"Yes, her sufferings are over. Let us hope she is better off. My boy, I think you had better return to your bed. You can do nothing for your mother now."

"I would rather stay here," said Frank, sadly. "I can at least look at her, and soon I shall lose even that comfort."

The thought was too much for the poor boy, and he burst into tears.

"Do as you please, Frank," assented Mr. Manning. "I feel for you, and I share in your grief. I will go and tell Mark of our sad loss."

He made his way to Mark's chamber and entered. He touched Mark, who was in a doze, and he started up.

"What's the matter?" he asked, crossly.

"Your poor mother is dead, Mark."

"Well, there was no need to wake me up for

that," said the boy, irritably. "I can't help it, can I?"

"I think, my son, you might speak with more feeling. Death is a solemn thing."

"There's nobody here but me," said Mark, sneering.

"I don't catch your meaning," said his father, showing some annoyance, for it is not pleasant to be seen through.

"Why should you care so much?" continued Mark. "I suppose you will be well provided for. Do you know how she has left the property? How much of it goes to Frank?"

"I can't say," said Mr. Manning. "I never asked my wife."

"Do you mean to say, father, that you don't know how the property is left?" asked Mark, with a sharp glance at his father.

"I may have my conjectures," said Mr. Manning, softly. "I don't think my dear wife would leave me without some evidences of her affection. Probably the bulk of the estate goes to your brother, and something to me. Doubtless we shall continue to live here, as I shall naturally be your brother's guardian."

"Don't call him my brother," said Mark.

"Why not? True, he is only your step-brother; but you have lived under the same roof, and been to school together, and this ought to strengthen the tie between you."

"I don't like Frank," said Mark. "He puts on altogether too many airs."

"I had not observed that," said his father.

"Well, I have. Only this evening he saw fit to speak impudently to me."

"Indeed! I am really amazed to hear it," said Mr. Manning, softly.

"Oh, he thinks he is the master of the house, or will be," said Mark, "and he presumes on that."

"He is unwise," said Mr. Manning. "Even if the whole property descends to him, which I can hardly believe possible, I, as his guardian, will have the right to control him."

"I hope you'll do it, father. At any rate, don't let him boss over me, for I won't stand it."

"I don't think he will boss over you," answered his father, in a slow, measured voice, betraying, however, neither anger nor excitement. "Of course, I should not permit that."

Mark regarded his father fixedly.

"I guess the old man knows what's in the will," he said to himself. "He knows how to feather his own nest. I hope he's feathered mine, too."

Mr. Manning passed from his son's chamber and went softly upstairs, looking thoughtful.

Any one who could read the impassive face would have read trouble in store for Frank.

CHAPTER IV.

MRS. MANNING'S WILL.

DURING the preparations for the funeral Frank was left pretty much to himself.

He spent most of his time in the chamber where his mother lay dead, waiting with a painful sense of bereavement for the solemn moment when the form of her whom he tenderly loved should be laid away in the grave.

He regarded the future with apathy. As a matter of course, his stepfather would be his guardian, but he didn't apprehend any troublesome interference with his liberty.

Mr. Manning's manner was so soft, and to him had been so deferential, that he did not understand the man. It didn't occur to him that it was assumed for a purpose.

That manner was not yet laid aside. His stepfather offered to comfort him, but Frank listened in silence. Nothing that Mr. Manning could say had the power to lighten his load of grief. So far as words could console him, the sympathy of Deborah and the coachman, both old servants, whom his mother trusted, had more effect, for he knew that it was sincere, and that they were really attached to his mother.

Of Mr. Manning he felt a profound distrust, which no words of his could remove.

As to Mark, he was not old enough to put on the mask, and went about the house studying his own comfort, and looking out for his own selfish interests.

"I shall be glad when the funeral is over," he said, impatiently. "The whole house seems to be upset. I can't get a decent meal."

Deborah, to whom this was addressed, responded, indignantly:

"You haven't any more feeling than a stone, Mr. Mark, so you haven't, or you wouldn't talk so while that dear lady, who has always been so kind to you, lies dead upstairs."

"I can't help it, can I?" said the boy, sullenly.

"No; but you can behave decently for the short time we shall have her with us."

"I ain't going to be lectured by a servant," said Mark, insolently.

"Servants have some rights," said Deborah, independently. "Why can't you imitate Master Frank? He isn't half so hard to please as you, though he is the owner of the property."

"Is he, though?" demanded Mark, with a sneer.

"To be sure he is!"

"He won't be the master of the house, though—I can tell you that!"

"Who will be?"

"My father."

"Who told you that?" asked Deborah, keenly.

"There is no need of anybody telling me it. Of course my father will be Frank's guardian, and he'll make him stand round, you may depend on that."

Deborah looked significantly at the coachman, suspecting that Mark had had some hint from his father.

"We can tell better after the will is read," she said, coldly.

As Mark left the room, she said to the coachman:

"I am afraid trouble is in store for Mr. Frank. I can't help thinking Mr. Manning is up to some trick."

"Shouldn't wonder at all," said Richard Green. "It would be just like him. But Master Frank isn't the one to be cheated without making a fuss about it."

"Little he thinks about the property now, poor boy," said Deborah. "That boy's heart was wrapped up in his mother, and she was always thinking of him. Why should she be taken, and such a poor creature as her husband be left?"

"It isn't always the good that live longest," said Richard, sententiously. "To my mind, it seems to be pretty much the other way. I expect Mark will give us a good deal of trouble."

"Like father, like son," said Deborah.

"The boy's a good deal worse than his father. Mr. Manning likes to have things his own way, but he's soft-spoken, while Mark is rough and impudent."

"I hope he will go off to schoool, and stay there. We can do better without him than with him," said Deborah.

Meanwhile, Mr. Manning was looking from an upper window down the fine avenue, and his eye ranged from left to right over the ample estate with a glance of self-complacent triumph.

"All mine at last!" he said to himself, exultantly. "What I have been working for has come to pass. Three years ago I was well-nigh penniless, and now I am a rich man. I shall leave Mark the master of a great fortune. I have played my cards well. No one will suspect anything wrong. My wife and I have lived in harmony. There will be little wonder that she has left all to me. There would be, perhaps, but for the manner in which I have taken care he shall be mentioned in the will—I mean, of course, in the will I have made for her."

He paused, and, touching a spring in the wall, a small door flew open, revealing a shallow recess.

In this recess was a folded paper, tied with a red ribbon.

Mr. Manning opened it, and his eyes glanced rapidly down the page.

"This is the true will," he said to himself. "I wish I could summon courage to burn it.

It would be best out of the way. That, if found out, would make me amenable to the law, and I must run no risk. In this secret recess it will never be found. I will replace it, and the document which I have had prepared will take its place, and no one will be the wiser."

On the day after the funeral, the family solicitor and a few intimate friends, who had been invited by Mr. Manning, assembled in the drawing room of the mansion to hear the will read.

Mr. Manning himself notified Frank of the gathering and its object.

He found our hero lying on the bed in his chamber, sad and depressed.

"I don't like to intrude upon your grief, my dear boy," said his stepfather, softly, "but it is necessary. The last will of your dear mother and my beloved wife is about to be read, and your presence is necessary."

"Couldn't it be put off?" asked Frank, sadly. "It seems too soon to think of such things."

"Pardon me, my dear Frank, but it is quite needful that there should be an immediate knowledge of the contents of the will, in order that the right person may look after the business interests of the estate. I assure you that it is the invariable custom to read the will immediately after the funeral."

"If that is the custom, and it is necessary,

I have nothing to say. When is the will to be read?"

"At three o'clock, and it is now two."

"Very well, sir; I will come down in time."

"Of course there can't be much doubt as to the contents of the will," pursued Mr. Manning. "You are doubtless the heir, and as you are a minor, I am probably your guardian. Should such be the case, I hope that the relations between us may be altogether friendly."

"I hope so," said Frank, gravely.

At three o'clock the members of the family, with a few outside friends, gathered in the drawing room. The family solicitor, Mr. Ferret, held in his hand what purported to be the last will of Mrs. Manning.

The widowed husband had directed the lawyer to the bureau of the deceased lady as likely to contain her will. It was found without trouble in the topmost drawer.

Deborah and the coachman had speculated as to whether they would be invited to attend at the reading of the will.

Their doubts were set at rest by an invitation from Mr. Manning himself.

"You were so long in the service of my dear wife," he said, "that it is fitting that you should be present at the reading of her will, in which it is quite probable that you may be personally interested."

"He is uncommonly polite, I am sure," thought Deborah, disposed for the moment to think more favorably of the man whom she had never been able to like.

"My friends," said the lawyer, after a preliminary cough, "you are assembled to listen to the will of Mrs. Manning, just deceased The document which I hold in my hand I believe to be such an instrument. I will now open it for the first time."

He untied the ribbon, and began reading the will.

It commenced with the usual formula, and proceeded to a few bequests of trifling amount.

Deborah and Richard Green were each left two hundred dollars," as a slight acknowledgment of their faithful service."

One or two friends of the family were remembered, but to an inconsiderable extent. Then came the important clause:

"All the rest and residue of the property of which I may die possessed I leave to my beloved husband, James Manning, whose devoted affection has made happy the last years of my life. Having implicit confidence in his good judgment and kindness of heart, I request him to make proper provision for my dear son Frank, whose happiness I earnestly desire. I hope that he will consent to be guided by the wisdom and experience of his stepfather, who, I am sure, will study his interests and counsel him wisely. In my sorrow at parting with my dear son, it is an unspeakable comfort to me to feel that he will have such a guardian and protector."

Frank listened with amazement, which was shared by all present.

Practically, he was disinherited, and left wholly dependent upon his stepfather.

CHAPTER V.

DISINHERITED.

THE contents of the will created general astonishment. There was not one in the room who didn't know the devotion of Mrs. Manning to her son Frank, yet, while speaking of him affectionately, she had treated him, as they considered, most cruelly. Why should she have left such a dangerous power in her husband's hands?

And how was Mr. Manning affected?

He summoned to his face an expression of bewilderment and surprise, and, feeling that all eyes were fixed upon him, he turned toward the lawyer.

"Mr. Ferret," he said, "I need hardly say that this will surprises me very much, as I see that it does the friends who are present. Are you sure that there is no codicil?"

"I have been unable to discover any, Mr. Manning," said the lawyer, gravely, as he scanned the face of the widower keenly.

Mr. Manning applied his handkerchief to his eyes, and seemed overcome by emotion.

"I knew my dear wife's confidence in me," he said, in a tremulous voice, "but I was not prepared for such a striking manifestation of it."

"Nor I," said Mr. Ferret, dryly.

"Knowing her strong attachment to Frank," pursued Mr. Manning, "I feel the full extent and significance of that confidence when she leaves him so unreservedly to my care and guidance. I hope that I may be found worthy of the trust."

"I hope so, sir," said Mr. Ferret, who, sharp lawyer as he was, doubted whether all was right, and was willing that Mr. Manning should be made aware of his feeling. "It is cetainly a very remarkable proviso, considering the affection which your wife entertained for her son."

"Precisely, Mr. Ferret. It shows how much confidence the dear departed felt in me."

"So far as I can see, the boy is left wholly dependent upon you."

"He shall not regret it!" said Mr. Manning, fervently. "I consecrate my life to this sacred trust."

"You acquiesce in the arrangement, then, Mr. Manning?"

"I cannot do otherwise, can I?"

"There is nothing to prevent you settiing the property, or any part of it, on the natural heir, Mr. Manning. You must pardon me for saying that it would have been wiser had your wife so stipulated by will."

"I cannot consent to reverse, or in any way annul, the last wishes of my dear wife," said Mr. Manning, hastily. "It was her arrangement solely, and I hold it sacred. She has put upon me a serious responsibility, from which I shrink, indeed, but which I cannot decline. I will do all in my power to carry out the wishes of my late wife."

Mr. Ferret shrugged his shoulders.

"I am not surprised at your decision, sir," he said, coldly. "Few men would resist the temptation. My duty is discharged with the reading of the will, and I will bid you good-afternoon!"

"My dear sir," said Mr. Manning, fervently, "permit me to thank you for the service you have rendered! Permit me also to express my high appreciation of your professional character and attainments, and to say that I hope you will allow me to call them into requisition should I hereafter have need to do so!"

Mr. Ferret acknowledged this compliment coldly enough.

He merely bowed.

With a general bow to the company, in which sauvity and deference were combined, Mr. Manning left the room, followed by Mark.

He was a crafty man. He knew that the

strange will would be discussed and he thought it best that the discussion should come at once, that it might be the sooner finished.

Deborah, faithful old servant, was in a blaze of indignation.

She went up quickly to Frank, and said:

"It's a shame, Mr. Frank, so it is!"

"If my mother made that will, it is all right," said Frank, gravely.

"But she didn't, Mr. Frank! I know she would never do such a thing. She loved you as the apple of her eye, and she would not cheat you out of your rightful inheritance."

"No more she would, Mr. Frank," said the coachman, chiming in.

"I don't know what to think," said Frank. "It has surprised me very much."

"Surprised you!" exclaimed Deborah. "You may well say that. You might have knocked me down with a feather when I heard the property left away from you. Depend upon it, that man knows all about it."

"You mean Mr. Manning?"

"To be sure I mean him! Oh, he's managed artfully! I say that for him. He's got it all into his own hands, and you haven't a cent."

"If it was my mother's will I wouldn't complain of that, Deborah. It was hers to do with as she liked, and I know, at any rate, that she loved me."

"There's one thing surprises me," said

Richard Green. "If so be as the will isn't genuine, how does it happen that you and I come in for a legacy, Deborah?"

"It's meant for a blind," answered Deborah. "Oh, he's the artfulest man!"

"You may be right, Deborah. I must say the will sounded all right."

"Maybe it was copied from the mistress' will."

This conversation took place in one corner of the room.

It ceased as Mr. Ferret advanced toward the disinherited boy.

"Frank," said he, in a tone of sympathy, "I am very sorry for the provisions of the will."

"So am I, sir," answered our hero. "It isn't pleasant to be dependent on Mr. Manning."

"Particularly when the whole estate should be yours."

"I wouldn't have minded if half had been left to him, provided I had been left independent of him."

"I appreciate your feelings, Frank. I knew your father, and I am proud to say that he was my friend. I knew your mother well, and I esteemed her highly. I hope you will let me regard myself as your friend also."

"Thank you, Mr. Ferret!" said Frank. "I am likely to need a friend. I shall remember your kind proposal. I want to ask you one question."

"Ask, and I shall answer."

"Did my mother consult with you about making this will?"

"No, Frank."

"Did she ever say anything that would lead you to think she would leave the property as it is left in this will?"

"Not a word."

"Was there another will?"

"Yes. I wrote her will at her direction more than a year ago. This will is dated only three months since, and, of course, takes precedence of it, even if the other is in existence."

"Can you tell me what were the provisions of the other will?"

"A legacy of ten thousand dollars was left to Mr. Manning, and the rest of the estate to you, except the small legacies, which were all larger than in the will I have read. For instance, Deborah and Richard Green were each put down for five hundred dollars."

"So they suffer as well as I?"

"Yes."

"Have you any idea, Mr. Ferret, of the value of the estate which falls into Mr. Manning's hands?"

"I have some idea, because I have talked with your mother on the subject. This estate is worth fifty thousand dollars at least, and there are fully fifty thousand dollars in money and bonds. The legacies do not altogether exceed one thousand dollars, and therefore it may be said that your stepfather has fallen heir to one hundred thousand dollars."

"I suppose there is nothing I can do, Mr. Ferret?"

"Not unless you can show that this will which I have read is not a genuine document. That would be difficult."

"Did you notice my mother's signature?"

"Yes. I am not an expert, but I cannot detect any difference greater than maybe existed between two signatures of the same person."

"Then I suppose there is nothing to be done at present. I expect to have a hard time with Mr. Manning, Mr. Ferret."

"How has he treated you in the past, Frank?" asked the lawyer.

"I have had nothing to complain of; but then he was not master of the estate. Now it is different, and I think his treatment of me will be different."

"You may be right. You remember what I said, Frank?"

"That I should regard you as a friend? I won't forget it, Mr. Ferret."

One by one the company left the house, and Frank was alone.

Left alone and unsustained by sympathy,

he felt more bitterly than before the totally unexpected change in his circumstances.

Up to the last hour he had regarded himself as the heir of the estate. Now he was only a dependent of a man whom he heartily disliked.

Could it be that this misfortune had come to him through the agency of his mother?

"I will not believe it!" he exclaimed, energetically.

He felt that he would be the better for a breath of fresh air. He sauntered slowly down the avenue, when a sight greeted him which kindled his indignation.

His stepbrother, Mark Manning, was riding, a little distance in advance, upon his horse—a horse which, two years before, his mother had given him.

His eyes flashed, and he hurried forward to overtake him.

CHAPTER VI.

AJAX.

A FEW words by way of explanation will be in place.

Among those who heard the will read was Mark Manning. Though he felt little interest in his stepmother, he was very much interested in learning the disposition of her property.

Had it fallen to Frank, he would have been

very much annoyed, as this would have made a great gulf between them. As the heir of a large property, Frank would be of infinitely more consequence than a penniless boy like himself, or be likely to think himself so, and this the jealous spirit of Mark Manning could ill brook.

His gratified amazement may be conjectured when he heard the will read, and found that Frank himself was the penniless boy, while he was the son and heir of the possessor of the estate.

A boy with a conscience might have felt some compunction at the grievous wrong which his stepbrother had suffered, but Mark was not the kind of boy to be troubled by such considerations. He felt a thrill of exultation which he did not even attempt to conceal.

Had Frank looked at his stepbrother, he would have seen the expression of triumph in his eyes, but our hero was too much occupied with his own sad reflections to look about the room.

"The old man has feathered his nest well," thought Mark. "Oh, he's sly as a fox, father is. You won't catch him napping. Master Frank will find his wings pretty well clipped. He can't fly very high now. He will have to look to father and me for support. I never felt so happy in my life."

Had Mr. Manning been a good, conscientious man, Mark would not have felt half so proud of him as at that moment. Young as he was, the boy idolized success, however attained, and felt that it was well to get rich, however questionable the means.

"He does it well," thought Mark, when his father, at the close of the reading, expressed his surprise at the disposition of the property. "Oh, he's a sly old fox!" he chuckled, inwardly. "He's a great man, father is."

When Mr. Manning left the room, Mark followed him.

He was impatient to congratulate him upon his success.

Mr. Manning made his way upstairs to the chamber where he spent much of his time. He was about to close the door when Mark came up.

"Is it you, Mark?" he asked, softly.

"Yes, father. May I come in?"

"Certainly, Mark. I have been very much surprised by the will, Mark."

"There's nobody here but me, father," said Mark, with a meaning smile.

"I don't understand you, my son."

"I mean that you have been very smart, father. I congratulate you."

"I am certainly glad of your good opinion, Mark," said the arch dissembler, who was not willing to lift the mask, even in the presence of his own son; "but really I am afraid I don't deserve your compliment, if you mean that I knew anything about the disposition of the property."

"Have it as you please, father. I suppose it is best to know nothing about it. How did you manage it?"

"Mark!" said his father, sharply, "let me warn you to cease speaking in this manner. It is not safe. Let it be supposed that I exercised undue influence over the mind of your stepmother, and an attempt would be made by Frank to upset the will. If his lawyer could make a jury believe that the charge was well founded, the attempt would be successful, and I need not say that your position, as well as mine, would be very materially altered.

Mark was sensibly impressed by this view of the case. The prospect of having the property snatched away, however remote, alarmed him, and he understood that he must be prudent.

"You are right, father," he said. "It's nothing to me how the property came to you, but I'm glad you've got it. How much are you going to give me?"

"Ahem! you will share in the advantage of it," said his father.

"Won't you give me ten thousand dollars down?" asked Mark.

"If I did, I should feel obliged to do the same for Frank."

"I don't see why."

"We don't wish to make talk, and as it is,

a great deal will be said about the will. Be patient, my son. When I am gone, you will be well provided for."

"But you may live a long time, and I should like to feel safe," said Mark.

Mr. Manning was not thin-skinned nor sensitive, but the cold-blooded selfishness of his son did stir him a little.

"You must have confidence in me, Mark," he said, rather coldly. "You are my only son. You are all I have to live for. You need not be afraid that you will suffer neglect."

"Are we going back to school—Frank and I?" asked Mark.

"I don't know; that will be decided in due time. Don't you want to go?"

"Well, I don't mind finishing the term, but now you have a fortune it is not necessary that I should study so hard. I shall have enough to live upon."

"I suppose the same may be said of your stepbrother."

"He isn't your son, and will have to take what you choose to give him. Of course I am your son and heir."

Mr. Manning coughed.

"You seem to forget, Mark," he said, "that the property came from Frank's mother."

"She gave it to you, didn't she?"

"Yes, but——"

"Then it is yours now. It makes no difference whom it used to belong to."

Mr. Manning smiled.

"Mark will know how to take care of himself," he thought. "He is very shrewd."

Just then Mark's thoughts were turned in a different direction.

Looking from the window, he saw Frank's horse grazing near the stable.

This horse had been given to our hero as a birthday gift a couple of years previous. He was a handsome animal, and Frank was very proud of him. He had become an excellent horseman, and when at home was often seen galloping over the country roads.

Mark could ride, but not so well. He had no horse of his own, and more than once had envied Frank his possession of his spirited steed. But his father had objected to buying him one.

"You must remember, Mark," he said, "that I have very little money of my own. Mrs. Manning is abundantly able to buy a horse for Frank, but you are not her son. You'll have to wait."

With this arrangement Mark was, as may be supposed, far from satisfied. He had no resource, however, but to accept his father's advice.

Now, however, as his glance fell upon the horse, he felt that the time had come for a change. It would never do for Frank to have a horse. while he, Mr. Manning's heir, was without one.

"Now you can give me a horse, father," he said.

"There are horses enough in the stable, Mark. It costs a good deal of money to keep so many. I feel more like selling a horse than buying another. I have a good income, but no money to throw away."

"Then is Frank to have a horse and I none at all?" demanded Mark.

"Frank has no horse," said Mr. Manning, coolly.

"Isn't Ajax his horse?"

"He calls him so, but he has no legal title to him. The will, in leaving the property to me, makes no exception in the case of the horse. I shall have to feed him, and he is therefore mine."

"Then give him to me, father," said Mark, eagerly.

"I can't do that. There would be the same objection to your owning him."

"I can ride him, though, can't I?"

"If I decide to keep him. One horse is enough for you and Frank."

"Frank will be mad!" said Mark, in a tone of satisfaction. "He never would let me ride Ajax—that is, not often."

"It is not for him to say now," said Mr. Manning.

"I mean to have my share of riding, now," said Mark. "I will go out this very afternoon!"

"Hadn't you better wait till to-morrow, Mark?"

"No time like the present, father. I'll have a fine gallop."

Before his father could object, he was out of the house and at the stable, where Richard Green had resumed his duties.

"Richard," said Mark, in a tone of authority, "saddle Ajax; I am going to ride."

"Does Mr. Frank say you can ride him?" asked the coachman.

"It is no business of Frank's," said Mark, haughtily.

"Isn't it his horse?"

"No, it isn't. It belongs to my father."

"It was given to Mr. Frank on his birthday."

"Nothing was said about it in the will. Father says I may ride it whenever I please."

This was not exactly what Mr. Manning had said, but Mark was not a stickler for the truth.

"Mr. Frank will make a fuss," said Richard.

"Let him!" said Mark. "He can settle matters with my father. I want him saddled right off."

"I will obey orders, Mr. Mark, but I don't think it is right."

"That doesn't matter. My father is master here, and if he says I can ride Ajax, I will."

"There'll be trouble, I reckon," said the

coachman, as he saw Mark ride out of the yard.

CHAPTER VII.

MARK'S DISCOMFITURE.

FRANK'S indignation was aroused when he saw Mark Manning on his favorite steed, and he hurried forward till he was near enough to be heard by his stepbrother.

"What are you doing on that horse, Mark Manning?" he demanded, sternly.

Mark had always been a little afraid of Frank, who, as he had reason to know, excelled him in physical strength. Now, backed by the knowledge that Frank was less favorably situated than himself as regards property, he felt an increase of courage, and disposed to be defiant.

"I am riding," he answered, shortly.

"And what business have you to be riding my horse without permission?" demanded Frank, with flashing eyes.

"He is not your horse," retorted Mark.

"What do you mean by that?" said Frank, beginning to suspect that there was something underneath which he did not understand.

"I suppose you heard the will, didn't you?"

"Well?"

"Was anything said in the will about Ajax going to you?"

"Oh, that's it, is it?" returned Frank, his

lip curling. "Did you take out my horse with your father's knowledge?"

"What has that to do with it?"

"Did you ask him if you might use it?"

"Suppose I did?"

"Does he say Ajax does not belong to me?"

"Yes, he does. I hope you are satisfied now."

"So, not content with robbing me of the estate, he must even take my birthday gift," said Frank, bitterly.

"You'd better not say that he robbed you of the estate," said Mark, concluding that Frank was inclined to yield.

"You'd better get off that horse!" said Frank, angrily.

Mark hesitated, but inclination, and the thought that his father would back him, decided him to hold out.

"Good-by!" said he, with mock politeness, raising his hat. "I'm off!"

"Ajax!" called Frank, quickly.

Our hero had perfect control over his horse. As a rider, he was at once fearless and kind, and the steed was attached to him.

No sooner did he hear Frank's voice than he turned at once, and, in spite of Mark's pulling at the rein, advanced to Frank and rubbed his nose against his hand.

"Good fellow!" said Frank, stroking him.

Mark was humiliated by his inability to control the animal, and colored with anger and vexation.

"Let go that horse, Frank Courtney!" he ordered.

"It strikes me that you had better get off," said Frank, coolly.

"You will repent this!" exclaimed Mark, furiously.

"Let me advise you hereafter not to interfere with my property," said Frank.

Mark twitched the reins angrily, and, raising his whip, lashed the horse. It was an unfortunate experiment.

Ajax disliked Mark as much as he liked his master, and, on feeling the lash, reared and plunged, while his rider turned pale and clung to his seat in an ecstasy of terror.

The truth must be told that Mark possessed very little physical courage, and found his position very uncomfortable.

"Stop making the horse plunge!" he exclaimed, almost breathless.

Frank smiled. It was not in human nature not to enjoy the discomfiture of his rival.

"You brought it on yourself," he said, coolly. "Why did you strike him?"

By this time Ajax had become quiet, and Mark made haste to slide off his back.

"I'll tell my father how you spoiled my ride!" he said, angrily.

"Do so, if you like," said Frank, contemptuously. "If you allude to the conduct of the horse, it is your own fault."

"He was acting well enough till you came up!" said Mark, angrily.

"You'd better not attempt to ride him again. Then you will have no reason to complain."

"If I don't ride him, you shan't!" retorted Mark.

"Who's going to prevent me?"

"My father will prevent you."

Frank had not intended to ride. He was in no mood to do so while his loss was so recent, but he was provoked by the words and behavior of Mark, and his answer was to leap on the back of Ajax and turn his head down the avenue, before his stepbrother had divined his intention.

Mark saw the tables so completely turned upon him that he screamed:

"Come back here, if you know what is best for yourself!"

"You must be crazy!" said Frank, and deigned no further notice of his stepbrother's anger.

"I'll be even with him for this—see if I don't!" muttered Mark, as he slowly took his way back to the house.

On the way he met Richard Green, the coachman.

The latter stopped short, and asked him, in surprise:

"What have you done with Ajax, Mr. Mark?"

"What have I done with him?" repeated Mark. "I'd like to shoot him."

"Why, what's the matter?"

"If you must know, Frank set him to rearing and plunging so that it was not safe to ride him."

"And you got off."

"Yes."

"Why didn't you bring him back?"

"Because I didn't choose to."

"Did Mr. Frank get on his back?"

"Yes."

"Oh, I understand!" said Richard, with a significant smile, that angered and mortified Mark.

"Perhaps you don't understand as much as you suppose!" he retorted. "I don't think he ll ride the horse again very soon."

"I thought there'd be trouble," soliloquized the coachman, as he went back to the stable, "and that Mr. Frank wouldn't come off second best. This is only the beginning. That boy Mark means to kick up a fuss, and I mistrust he and his father together will make the house pretty uncomfortable. All the same, I am glad Mr. Frank got back his horse."

Mark could not wait for his anger to cool. He straightway sought his father, and proceeded to prefer complaints against Frank, taking care to make his case as strong as possible without strict adherence to the truth.

"You say that Frank tried to make the horse throw you?" inquired his father.

"To be sure he did. He was very angry because I presumed to use him."

"Did you tell him that you had my permission, Mark?"

"Yes, I did; but it made no difference. He hasn't the slightest respect for you."

Mr. Manning's voice was not quite so soft as usual as he said:.

"He had better have a care. I do not propose to indulge him as his mother did. Of one thing he may rest assured— that I intend to be master in this house and on this estate."

"Good for you, father! I thought you wouldn't knuckle down to a mere boy like him," said Mark, artfully trying to fan the flames of his father's resentment.

Mr. Manning smiled, but the smile was not a pleasant one.

"Probably Frank does not understand me," he said. "During his mother's life I forbore to assert myself or my authority out of regard for her feelings. I saw much in Frank's conduct and manners that I could not approve, but I put a restraint upon myself for the sake of my dear wife. I believe I made her happy, and at this hour I feel repaid for all my sacrifices."

He was about to relapse into a sentimental mood, but Mark did not sympathize with it. He chose to construe his father's words in a way not intended.

"Yes, father, you are well repaid. You are a rich man now."

"That was not exactly what I intended to convey, Mark," said his father, coughing.

"Well, it don't matter. You can do as you please now, and I hope you'll make Frank keep his place."

"You may be assured that I will," said his father, compressing his thin lips. "When Frank comes in, will you send him to me, if you see him?"

"I will make it my business to see him," said Mark, in a tone of satisfaction. "Just give it to him red-hot, father!"

"Mark, I am shocked at your expression. It is not refined."

Mark shrugged his shoulders and left his father's presence, not particularly mortified by the rebuke. In fact, hard as it is to say it, he had rather a contempt for his father, though he believed in his sharpness and ability.

But Mark saw through him. He understood very well that his parent was an arch-dissembler and a hypocrite, and for such a man even he could not feel respect.

He lay in wait till Frank returned from his ride, and greeted him thus:

"My father wants to see you right off."

"Where is your father?"

"In his room."

"I will go up to him," answered Frank, gravely. "I, too, wish to see him!"

CHAPTER VIII.

AN UNSATISFACTORY INTERVIEW.

FRANK entered the room in which his stepfather sat. His air was manly and his bearing that of a boy who respects himself, but there was none of the swagger which some boys think it necessary to exhibit when they wish to assert their rights.

Mr. Manning, in a flowered dressing gown, sat at a table, with a sheet of paper before him and a lead pencil in his hand. Short as had been the interval since his accession to the property, he was figuring up the probable income he would derive from the estate.

He looked up as Frank entered the room, and surveyed him with cold and sarcastic eyes. His soft tones were dropped.

"Mr. Manning," said Frank, "I wish to ask you a question."

"And I wish to ask you a question," said his stepfather. "Odd coincidence, isn't it?" he added, with a sneer.

"Very well, sir," said Frank, in no wise daunted by his manner. "As you are the older, I will first listen to what you have to say."

"You are very considerate, I am sure," said Mr. Manning, with an unpleasant smile. "Let me ask you, in a word, to explain your outrageous treatment of Mark."

"What does he say I have done?"

"It is hardly necessary to answer that question, since you know very well what you have done."

"I know very well what I have done, but I don't know what he may choose to say I have done."

"Do you mean to charge him with untruth?"

"Not until I know whether he has made a misstatement."

"He says you caused Ajax to rear and plunge, and so compelled him to dismount."

"Did he mention that he kicked the horse, and that this was the cause of the horse's behavior?"

"No."

"Then he omitted a very important part of the truth."

"Did you do nothing to incite the horse to his bad behavior?"

"No, sir. I called the horse by name, and he responded."

"Humph! I begin to understand. Would Mark have had any difficulty with the horse had you not been present?"

"Perhaps not."

"So I thought," exclaimed Mr. Manning, triumphantly.

"Please wait till I have finished, sir," said Frank, calmly. "In that case, Mark would probably not have struck the horse. That caused him to rear."

"By your own confession, your presence occasioned all the difficulty," said Mr. Manning, perversely. "Did you not order him to get off the horse?"

"Yes, sir."

"After he had told you that he had taken it from the stable by my permission?"

"Yes, sir."

"Then you defied my authority," said Mr. Manning, sternly. "What excuse have you for this?"

"You seem to have forgotten, Mr. Manning," said Frank, calmly, "that the horse was a birthday present to me."

"That meant only that you were to have the chief use of it. Was the horse left to you in the will?"

"There was very little reference to me in the will," said Frank, bitterly.

"So you would complain of your poor mother, would you?" said his stepfather, in a tone of virtuous indignation.

"I cannot believe that my mother made that will."

Mr. Manning colored. He scented danger. Should Frank drop such hints elsewhere, he might make trouble, and lead to a legal investigation, which Mr. Manning had every reason to dread.

"This is very foolish," he said, more mildly. "No doubt you are disappointed, but probably your mother has provided wisely. You will want for nothing, and you will be prepared for the responsibilities of manhood under my auspices."

Mr. Manning's face assumed a look of self-complacence as he uttered these last words.

"I have no blame to cast upon my dear mother," said Frank. "If she made that will, she acted under a great mistake."

"What mistake, sir?"

"She failed to understand you."

"Do you mean to imply that I shall be false to my trust?"

"Not at present, sir. I don't wish to judge of you too hastily. Now, may I ask my question?"

"You have not answered mine. But let that pass. Ask your question."

"Is Mark to share with me the use of Ajax?"

"Yes."

"Though he is my horse?"

"You are mistaken. He is my horse."

"Yours!" said Frank, hastily.

"Certainly. He comes to me with the rest of the property."

"And I have absolutely nothing," said Frank, bitterly.

"What does it matter? You and Mark will have the use of Ajax, while I pay for his feed. My ownership will bring me no advantage."

"I have nothing further to say, sir," said Frank, as he turned to go downstairs.

"But I have," said Mr. Manning.

"Very well, sir."

"I demand that you treat my son Mark with suitable respect, and forbear to infringe upon his rights."

Frank looked up, and answered, with spirit:

"I shall treat Mark as well as he treats me, sir. Is that satisfactory?"

"I apprehend," said Mr. Manning, "that you may make some mistakes upon that point."

"I will try not to do so, sir."

Frank left the room, and this time was not called back.

His stepfather looked after him, but his face expressed neither friendliness nor satisfaction.

"That boy requires taming," he said to himself. "He is going to make trouble. I must consider what I will do with him."

As Mr. Manning reviewed Frank's words, there was one thing which especially disturbed him—the doubt expressed by his stepson as to his mother's having actually made the will.

He saw that it would not do for him to go too far in his persecution of Frank, as it might drive the latter to consult a lawyer in regard to the validity of the will by which he had been disinherited.

When Frank left his stepfather's presence, he went out to the stable. There he found Richard Green, the coachman, who had general charge of the horses.

"Well, Mr. Frank," said Richard, smiling, "did you have a pleasant ride?"

"No, Richard; I had too much on my mind to enjoy it."

"Mr. Mark came back in a bad temper," chuckled the coachman.

"I suppose I interrupted his ride," said Frank.

"Served him right. What business has he to take out your horse?"

"Mr. Manning has just told me that it is not my horse."

"Whose is it, then, I'd like to know?"

"He says it is his, and that it was left to him with the property."

"There's no end to that man's impudence!" ejaculated Richard. "Didn't your mother give it to you for your birthday?"

"That appears to count for nothing, Richard. Mr. Manning says that Mark shall have the same use of it that I have."

"Are you going to submit to it, Mr. Frank?"

"I don't know yet what I shall do. I am likely to see a good deal of trouble. If my dear mother really made that will—which I can't believe—she little suspected how unhappy she was going to make me."

"She was too good to suspect the badness of others, Mr. Frank. She thought old Manning was really all that he pretended to be, and that he would be as kind to you as she was herself. When she was alive, he was always as soft as—as silk."

"His manner has changed now," said Frank, gravely. "Excuse me, Richard, for finding fault with you, but don't call him old Manning?"

"Why not, Mr. Frank?"

"I have no liking for Mr. Manning—in fact, I dislike him—but he was the husband of my mother, and I prefer to speak of him respectfully."

"I dare say you are right, Mr. Frank, but, all the same, he don't deserve it. Is Mr. Mark to ride Ajax, then?"

"If he asks for it, you are to saddle Ajax for him. I don't want you to get into any trouble with Mr. Manning on my account."

"I don't care for that, Mr. Frank. I can get another place, and I don't much care to serve Mr. Manning."

"I would rather you would stay, if you can, Richard. I don't want to see a new face in the stable."

"I don't think he means to keep me long, Mr. Frank. Deborah and I will have to go, I expect, and he'll get some servants of his own here."

"Has he hinted anything of this, Richard?" asked Frank, quickly.

"No; but he will soon, you may depend on it. I won't lose sight of you, though. I've known you since you were four years old, and I won't desert you, if I can do any good—nor Deborah, either."

"I have two friends, then, at any rate," said Frank to himself. "That is something."

CHAPTER IX.

A SCHOOL FRIEND.

EARLY Monday morning it had been the custom for Frank and Mark to take the train for Bridgeville, to enter upon a new week at the academy.

Frank felt that it would be better for him to go back without any further vacation, as occupation would serve to keep him from brooding over his loss.

"Are you ready, Mark?" he asked, as he rose from the breakfast-table.

"Ready for what?"

"To go back to school, of course."

"I am not going back this morning," answered Mark.

"Why not?" asked Frank, in some surprise.

"I am going to stay at home to help father," said Mark, with a glance at Mr. Manning.

"If I can be of any service to you, sir, I will stay, too," said Frank, politely.

"Thank you, but Mark will do all I require," replied his stepfather.

"Very well, sir."

Frank appeared at the academy with a grave face and subdued manner, suggestive of the great loss he had sustained From his schoolfellows, with whom he was a favorite, he received many words of sympathy—from none more earnest or sincere than from Herbert Grant.

"I know how you feel, Frank," he said, pressing the hand of his friend. "If I could comfort you I would, but I don't know how to do it."

"I find comfort in your sympathy," said Frank. "I look upon you as my warmest friend here."

"I am glad of that, Frank."

To Herbert alone Frank spoke of his mother and her devoted affection; but even to him he did not like to mention the will and his disinheritance. He did not so much lament the loss of the property as that he had lost it by the direction of his mother, or, rather, because it would generally be supposed so.

For himself, he doubted the genuineness of the will, but he felt that it was useless to speak of it, as he was unprepared with any proofs.

So it happened that when, on Wednesday afternoon, Mark Manning made his appearance, Frank's change of position, as respected the property, was neither known nor suspected by his schoolfellows. It was soon known, however, and of course, through Mark.

The boys immediately noticed a change in Mark. He assumed an air of consequence, and actually strutted across the campus. Instead of being polite and attentive to Frank, he passed him with a careless nod, such as a superior might bestow on an inferior.

"What has come over Mark?" asked Herbert of Frank, as the two were walking together from recitation.

"How do you mean?"

"He holds his head higher than he used to do. He looks as if he had been elected to some important office."

"You will soon learn, Herbert," said Frank. "Make a pretext to join him, and let the news come from him."

Herbert looked puzzled.

"Do you wish me to do this?" he asked.

"Yes, I have a reason for it."

"Very well. I am always ready to oblige you, Frank, but I hope Mark won't think I have suddenly formed a liking for his society."

"If he does, you can soon undeceive him."

"That is true."

Herbert left the side of his friend, and sauntered toward Mark.

As Herbert was known as Frank's especial friend, Mark was at first surprised, but quickly decided that his improved position had been communicated by Frank, and that Herbert was influenced by it. That is to say, he judged Herbert to be as mean and mercenary as himself.

Herbert's position was too humble to entitle him to much notice from Mark, but the latter was pleased with the prospect of detaching from Frank his favorite friend.

"You came back rather late, Mark," said Herbert.

"Yes," answered Mark, with an air of importance. "I remained at home a short time, to help my father in his accounts. You know the property is large, and there is a good deal to do."

"I should think that was Frank's place, to help about the accounts."

"Why?"

"The property is his, of course!"

"Did he tell you that?" asked Mark, sharply.

"He has not said a word about the property."

"No, I suppose not," said Mark, with a sneering laugh.

"Has anything happened? Didn't his mother leave as much as was expected?" went on Herbert, quite in the dark.

"Yes, she left a large estate, but she didn't leave it to him."

"To whom, then?"

"To my father!" replied Mark, with conscious pride. "Frank has nothing. He is entirely dependent upon father."

"Did his mother leave him nothing, then?" asked Herbert, in pained surprise.

"Nothing at all," assured Mark, complacently.

"That is very strange and unjust."

"I don't look upon it in that light," said

Mark, nettled. "My father knows what is best for him. He will provide for him just as his mother did before."

"But when Frank is of age, doesn't he come into possession of the estate then?"

"No, of course not. Didn't I tell you it belongs to father? Frank is a poor boy—as poor as you," said Mark, in a tone of evident satisfaction.

"Or you," added Herbert, pointedly.

"You are mistaken," said Mark, quickly. "I am father's heir."

"Suppose your father dies—how will the property go?"

"I suppose something will be left to Frank, unless my father leaves me the property, with directions to provide for him."

"Would you think that right and just?" demanded Herbert, indignantly.

"Of course I would. My stepmother knew what she was about when she made her will. I see you are surprised. You won't be quite so thick with Frank, now, I expect."

"Why shouldn't I be?"

"Because he is just as poor as you are. He never can help you."

"Mark Manning, I believe you are about the meanest boy I ever encountered, and you judge me by yourself!"

"Do you mean to insult me? Mind what you say!" blustered Mark, unpleasantly surprised at this outburst from a boy whom he expected would now transfer his allegiance from Frank to himself.

"I mean that you and your father have robbed Frank of his inheritance, and glory in it, and you think that I am mean enough to desert him because he is no longer rich. It makes no difference to me whether he is rich or poor. I think I like him all the better because he has been so badly treated. As for you, I despise you, and shall continue to, even if you get the whole of Frank's money."

"You forget that you are talking to a gentleman, you low-born mechanic!" said Frank, angrily.

"You a gentleman!" replied Herbert, contemptuously. "Then I never want to be one!"

He walked away, leaving Mark very much incensed.

"He is a fool!" muttered Mark. "When I am a rich man, he may repent having insulted me."

Herbert went back to Frank.

"Did he tell you?" asked Frank, quietly.

"Yes; and he actually appeared to think I would be ready to desert you because you were poor, and follow him about."

"I am not afraid of that, Herbert."

"I don't think Mark will have that idea any more. I gave him a piece of my mind, and left him very angry. But what does it all mean, Frank?"

"I know no more than you do, Herbert. I cannot understand it."

"What could have induced your mother to make such a will?"

"I cannot believe my poor mother ever made such a will; but, if she did, I am very sure that she was overpersuaded by my stepfather, who is one of the most plausible of men."

"What shall you do about it?"

"What can I do? I am only a boy. I have no proof, you know."

"How are you likely to be treated?"

"I have had a little foretaste of that."

And Frank related the incident about Ajax.

"It looks very bad for you, Frank," admitted Herbert, in a tone of sympathy.

"I don't so much care for the loss of the property, Herbert," said Frank, "but I am afraid I shall have all sorts of annoyances to endure from Mark and his father. But I won't anticipate trouble. I will do my duty, and trust that things will turn out better than I fear."

The next afternoon a letter was placed in Frank's hands. It was in a brown envelope, and directed in a cramped and evidently unpracticed hand, with which Frank was not familiar.

On opening it, a glance at the signature showed that it was from Richard Green, the coachman. It commenced:

"Dear Mr. Frank: This comes hoping you are well.

I have no good news to tell. Mr. Manning has sold your horse, Ajax, and he is to be taken away to-night. I thought you ought to know it, and that is why I take my pen in hand to write."

There was more, but this is all that was important.

Frank's face flushed with anger. He immediately went in search of Mark, who, he felt assured, knew of the sale.

CHAPTER X.

A NEW PLAN.

MARK was in his room, where Frank found him trying on a new necktie. Though decidedly plain, Mark fancied himself very good-looking, and spent no little time on personal adornment. In particular, he had a weakness for new neckties, in which he indulged himself freely.

When the boys came to the academy, the principal proposed that they should room together; but both objected, and Mark had a room to himself—no one caring to room with him.

"Take a seat, Frank," said Mark, condescendingly. "Is there anything I can do for you?"

"Yes," answered Frank. "I hear that your father has sold Ajax, or is intending to do so. Will you tell me if it is true?"

"I believe it is," answered Mark, indifferently.

"And what right has he to sell my horse?" demanded Frank, indignantly.

"You'd better ask him," said Mark, with provoking coolness.

"It is an outrage," said Frank, indignantly.

"As to that," said his stepbrother, "you can't expect father to be at the expense of feeding your horse."

"With my money?"

"The money is legally his. Besides, it is a vicious brute. I haven't forgotten how he treated me the other day."

"It was all your fault. Why did you lash him?"

"Horses were meant to be whipped," said Mark. "If they were not, what do we have whips for?"

"At any rate, Ajax gave you a lesson on the subject," said Frank, significantly. "Do you know to whom your father has sold Ajax?"

"To Col. Vincent, I believe."

"I am glad, at any rate, that he will have a good master."

"How did you learn about his being sold?" inquired Mark, in considerable curiosity.

Frank reflected that a true answer might get the coachman into trouble, and replied, guardedly:

"I prefer not to tell you."

"I don't need to be told," said Mark. "I am sure it was either Deborah or Richard Green who wrote you. Wasn't it?"

"You are at liberty to guess."

"You can't keep it from me. I will soon find out."

"Just as you please. I may have heard from your father, for aught you know."

"I know you didn't, for he cautioned me not to tell you."

"Indeed!" said Frank. "Did he give any reason for concealing it? It seems to me that, as Ajax was bought for me, I ought to be the first to be informed."

"Father said you would make a fuss, and it was just as well you should not know till the horse was gone. I will let him know that he has spies in the house."

"You are mean enough to do so, Mark Manning, I know very well. It will be better for you not to meddle with matters that don't concern you."

"You'd better not insult me," said Mark, angrily, "or it will be the worse for you."

Frank laughed.

"I am not easily frightened," he said. "I am prepared for the consequences of my actions."

Frank felt that there would be no advantage in prolonging the interview, or carrying on further a war of words.

He sought out his friend Herbert, and communicated to him this last infraction of his rights.

"It is too bad, Frank!" said his sympathizing friend.

"Yes, it is," said Frank, gravely; "but I fear it is only the beginning of annoyances. I don't believe I can ever live in any place with Mr. Manning or Mark."

"Will it be necessary?"

"I suppose so. I have no money, as you know. All has gone to him. Herbert, I tell you frankly, I envy you and your position."

"Though my father is a poor man?"

"Yes; for, at any rate, you have a peaceful home, and a father and mother who love you. I have a stepfather, who will do all he can to make me miserable."

"Would you be willing to work for your own support, Frank?"

"Yes; far rather than remain a dependent on Mr. Manning."

"Suppose you should run away," suggested Herbert.

Frank shook his head.

"I wouldn't do that except in case of extreme necessity. I know that if my mother knows what goes on here, it would grieve her for me to take such a step."

"Suppose your stepfather should consent to your leaving home?"

"Then I would do so gladly. I am willing to work, and I think I could make a living in some way."

"Why not ask him?"

Frank's face brightened.

"Thank you for the hint, Herbert," he said. "I will think of it, and I may act upon it."

Frank was naturally self-reliant and energetic. He was not disposed to shrink from the duties of life, but was ready to go forth to meet them. The idea which Herbert had suggested commended itself to him the more he thought of it.

In spite, therefore, of the news which he had received about Ajax, he resumed his cheerfulness, considerably to the surprise of Mark, whose natural suspicion led him to conjecture that Frank had some plan in view to circumvent his father.

" If he has, he'd better give it up," reflected Mark. " The old man's as sly as a fox. A raw boy like Frank can't get the better of him."

At the close of the week, both the boys went home. They were on board the same train and the same car, but did not sit together. When they reached the house, Mr. Manning was not at home.

Frank went out to the stable at once to see Richard Green, the coachman.

He found him, indeed, but he also found another man, a stranger, who appeared to be employed in the stable.

" Who is this, Richard? " asked Frank.

" My successor," answered the coachman.

" Are you going to leave? " asked Frank, hastily.

" Come out with me, Mr. Frank, and I will tell you," said Richard. " I've had notice to leave," he said, "and so has Deborah. It came last evening. Mr. Manning got a letter from Bridgeville—I know that, because I brought it home from the post office—which appeared to make him angry. He called Deborah and me and told us that he should not need our services any longer."

"Did he give you any reason?"

"Yes; he said that he could have our places filled for a good deal less money, and he had no doubt we could do as well elsewhere."

"He has filled your place pretty soon."

"Yes. This man came this morning. I think Mr. Manning had sent for him already. I told you the other day we should soon be discharged."

"I know it; but I can tell you what has hastened it."

"What, then?"

"Mark wrote his father that I had learned about the sale of Ajax, and that the information came from you or Deborah."

"I think it likely, Mr. Frank, for the old gentleman seemed mighty cool. I hope you won't take it too much to heart that Ajax is sold."

"I am not sure but I am glad of it," said Frank.

The coachman looked at him in surprise.

"I thought you would be very angry," he said.

"So I was at first, but he has been sold to a

man who will treat him well, and I shall be glad to think of that when I'm away from home."

"You don't mean to run away, Mr. Frank?"

"No; but I mean to get my stepfather's permission to go, if I can."

"Where do you mean to go, Mr. Frank?"

"Somewhere where I can earn my living, without depending upon anybody. You know very well, Richard, how miserable I should be to stay here in dependence upon Mr. Manning."

"But to think that you, to whom the property rightfully belongs, should go away and work for a living, while that man and his boy occupy your place. I can't bear to think of it."

"I have done a good deal of thinking within a few days, and I don't shrink from the prospect. I think I should rather enjoy being actively employed."

"But you were to go to college, Mr. Frank."

"I know it, Richard, but I am not sure whether it would be for the best. My tastes are for an active business life, and I don't care for a profession."

"Do you think your stepfather will give you a start?"

"In the way of money?"

"Yes."

"I don't know. If he won't, I have still fifty dollars in the savings-bank, which I have saved from my pocket money. I will take that."

"Mr. Frank, will you promise not to be offended at what I'm going to say?"

"I don't think you would say anything that ought to offend me, Richard."

"Then I want you to take the money that comes to me by the will—Mr. Manning is to pay it to me on Monday. I don't need it, and you may."

Frank shook his head.

"You are very kind, Richard, but I will get along with fifty dollars, unless Mr. Manning supplies me with more. If I really need money at any time, I will think of your offer."

"That's something, at any rate," said Richard, partly reconciled. "You won't forget it now, Mr. Frank?"

"No, Richard, I promise you."

Frank left the stable and went thoughtfully into the house.

CHAPTER XI.

THE NEW OWNER OF AJAX.

FRANK and Mark took supper alone, Mr. Manning having left word that he would not return till later in the evening.

After supper, Frank decided to go over to call upon Col. Vincent, the new owner of Ajax. His estate was distant about three-quarters of a mile from the Cedars.

As Frank started, Mark inquired:

"Where are you going, Frank?"

"To see Ajax," answered our hero.

"Do you mean to make any fuss about him? I wouldn't advise you to."

"Thank you for your advice."

"I wonder what he is going to do?" thought Mark. "Of course he can't do anything now."

He did not venture to propose to accompany Frank, knowing that his company would not be acceptable.

"Is Col. Vincent at home?" asked Frank, at the door of a handsome house.

"Yes, Mr. Courtney," replied the colored servant, pleasantly, for Frank was a favorite among all classes in the neighborhood. "Come right in, sir. De colonel am smoking a cigar on de back piazza."

Frank followed the servant through the hall which intersected the house, and stepped out on the back piazza.

A stout, elderly gentleman was taking his ease in a large rustic rocking-chair.

"Good-evening, Col. Vincent," our hero said.

"Good-evening, Frank, my boy," said the colonel, heartily. "Glad to see you. Haven't you gone back to school?"

"Yes, sir; but I came home to spend Sunday. It doesn't seem much like home now," he added, as his lip quivered.

"You have suffered a great loss, my dear boy," said the colonel, feelingly.

"The greatest, sir. My mother was all I had."

"I suppose Mr. Manning will keep up the establishment?"

"I suppose so, sir; but it is no longer home to me."

"Don't take it too hard, Frank. I was sorry about the will."

"So was I, sir; because it makes me dependent on a man whom I dislike."

"Don't be too prejudiced, Frank. I never took any fancy to your stepfather myself; but then we don't need to like everybody we associate with."

"I hear you have bought my horse, Col. Vincent," said Frank, desiring to change the subject.

"Was Ajax your horse?"

"Yes. It was given to me as a birthday present by my mother."

"I had some such idea, and expressly asked Mr. Manning whether the horse was not yours."

"What did he answer?"

"That it was only nominally yours, and that he thought it best to sell it, as both you and Mark were absent at school, and had no time to use it."

"I am not surprised at anything Mr. Manning may say," said Frank.

"It's too bad! I'll tell you what I will do, Frank. I haven't paid for the horse yet. I will return it to Mr. Manning, and tell him that I bought it under a misapprehension of the ownership. I don't think he will make any fuss."

"I would rather have you keep it, sir."

"You would!" exclaimed the colonel, in surprise.

"Yes, sir. If you should return Ajax, Mr. Manning would sell him to some one else, and you, I know, will treat him well."

"But you will lose the use of him. No, you won't, though. Come over to my stable when you like, and, if he is not in use, you can take him out."

"Thank you, sir! You are very kind. While I am in the neighborhood, I won't forget your kind offer. But I mean to go away."

"You mean to go away! Where?"

"Out into the world. Anywhere, where I can find work and make a living."

"But surely this is not necessary. Your stepfather will provide for you without your working."

"I have no reason to doubt it, Col. Vincent; but I shall be happier in the world outside."

"Of course you will let Mr. Manning know of your intention to leave home?"

"I shall ask his permission to go at the end of my school term. That comes in a couple of weeks."

"Where will you go?"

"A cousin of my father lives at Newark, New Jersey. I think I shall go to him first, and ask his advice about getting a place either there or in New York."

"You will need some money to start with. Do you think Mr. Manning will give you any?"

"I don't know, sir! That won't prevent my going. I have fifty dollars in a savings-bank, saved up from my allowance, and that will be all I shall need."

"If you have any difficulty on that score, Frank, remember that I was your father's friend, and mean to be yours. Apply to me at any time when you are in a strait."

"I will, sir, and thank you heartily."

"That was a strange will, Frank. I don't want to put any ideas into your head to disturb you, but had your mother ever led you to suspect that she intended to leave you dependent on your stepfather?"

"Never, sir!"

"Don't you think she would have done so, had she had such a plan in view?"

"I do," said Frank, quickly.

The colonel's eye met his, and each knew what the other suspected.

"There is nothing for me to do at present, sir," said Frank. "If Mr. Manning does not interfere with my plans, I shall not trouble him."

"I will hint as much when I see him. It may clear the way for you."

"I wish you would, sir."

"Come and see me again, Frank," said the colonel, as Frank rose to go.

"I certainly will, sir."

"Your father's son will always be welcome at my house. When did you say your school term closes?"

"In a fortnight."

"I will see your stepfather within a few days. By the way, Frank, wouldn't you like a gallop on Ajax to-night?"

"Yes, sir; I should enjoy it."

"Come out to the stable with me, then."

Ajax whinnied with delight when he saw his old, or rather his young master, and evinced satisfaction when Frank stroked him caressingly.

"Sam," said Col. Vincent, "Frank is to ride Ajax whenever he pleases. Saddle him for his use whenever he asks you."

"That I will, sir," answered Sam. "Often and often I've seen Mr. Frank on his back. Doesn't he ride well, though?"

"Don't flatter me, Sam," said Frank, laughing.

Five minutes later he was on the back of his favorite horse, galloping down the road.

"I hope I shall meet Mark," thought Frank. "I would like to give him a sensation."

Considering the manner in which Mark had treated his stepbrother, Frank may be excused for the wish to puzzle him a little.

Finding himself lonely, Mark decided to take a walk not long after Frank's departure. He was sauntering along the road, when he heard the sound of hoofs, and, to his surprise, saw his stepbrother on the back of Ajax.

His first thought was that Frank had gone to Col. Vincent's stable and brought away Ajax without permission, in defiance of Mr. Manning's will. He resolved to take him to task for it immediately. Frank purposely slackened the speed of his horse in order to give Mark the chance he sought.

"Why are you riding Ajax?" asked Mark.

"It is a pleasant evening," answered Frank, "and I thought I should enjoy it."

"Where did you get him?"

"From Col. Vincent's stable, where he never ought to have been carried," answered Frank, with spirit.

"You seem to think you can do anything you like, Frank Courtney," said Mark, provoked, deciding that his suspicions were well founded.

"Is there any particular reason why I should not ride Ajax?" demanded Frank.

"You have made yourself liable to arrest for horse stealing," said Mark. "It would serve you right if Col. Vincent should have you arrested and tried."

"I don't think he will gratify your kind wishes, Mark."

"Just wait and see what my father has to say to you."

"I have only done what I had a perfect right to do; but I can't stop to dispute with you. I must finish my ride. Hey, Ajax!"

As he spoke the horse dashed into a gallop,

and Mark was left looking after him in a disturbed frame of mind.

"I'll tell my father as soon as he gets home," he decided; and he kept his word.

In consequence, Frank, by that time returned, was summoned into Mr. Manning's presence.

"What's this I hear?" he began. "Did you ride Ajax this evening?"

"Yes, sir."

"Where did you find him?"

"In Col. Vincent's stable."

"This is a high-handed proceeding, Frank Courtney. Have you any excuse to offer?"

"None is needed, sir. Col. Vincent has given me permission to ride him whenever I please."

"It appears to me, Mark," said Mr. Manning, sharply, "that you have made a fool of yourself."

"How should I know?" replied Mark, mortified by the collapse of his sensation. "Frank didn't tell me he had leave to use the horse."

And he left the room, looking foolish.

CHAPTER XII.

MARK YIELDS TO TEMPTATION.

THERE are some boys, as well as men, who cannot stand prosperity.

It appeared that Mark Manning was one of these.

While his stepmother was living and his father's prospects—and consequently his own—were uncertain, he had been circumspect in his behavior and indulged in nothing that could be considered seriously wrong.

When his father came into possession of a large fortune, and his pocket-money was doubled, Mark began to throw off some of the restraint which, from motives of prudence, he had put upon himself.

About the middle of the next week, as Frank was taking a walk after school hours, he was considerably surprised to see Mark come out of a well-known liquor saloon frequented by men and boys of intemperate habits.

The students of Bridgeville Academy were strictly forbidden this or any other saloon, and I am sure that my boy readers will agree with me that this rule was a very proper one.

Mark Manning appeared to have been drinking. His face was flushed, and his breath, if one came near enough to him, was redolent of the fumes of alcohol. With him was James Carson, one of the poorest scholars and most unprincipled boys in the academy. It was rather surprising that he had managed for so long to retain his position in the institution, but he was crafty and took good care not to be caught.

To go back a little, it was chiefly owing to James Carson's influence that Mark had entered the saloon.

When he learned that Mark's worldly prospects had improved, and that he had a large supply of pocket money, he determined to cultivate his acquaintance—though privately he thought Mark a disagreeable boy—with the intention of obtaining for himself a portion of Mark's surplus means.

At the first of the term he had made similar advances to Frank, but they were coldly received, so much so that he did not think it worth while to persevere in courting our hero's intimacy.

He succeeded better with Mark, his crafty nature teaching him how to approach him.

"Mark," he said, with a great show of cordiality, "I am delighted to hear of your good fortune. I always liked you, and I think you deserve to be rich."

"Thank you!" said Mark, much gratified, for he liked flattery. "I am sure I am very much obliged to you."

"Oh, not at all! I only say what I think. Shall I tell you why I am particularly glad?"

"Yes, if you like," returned Mark, in some curiosity.

"Because I like you better than that young muff, your stepbrother. I hope you won't be offended at my plain speaking," he added, artfully.

"Certainly not!" said Mark, almost as well pleased with abuse of Frank as with praise of himself. "To tell you the truth, I don't much like Frank myself. He is my stepbrother, to be sure, but he always makes himself disagreeable to me."

"Then you are not offended with me?"

"Of course not! How can I expect you to like Frank, when I don't myself?"

Of course James was perfectly aware of the feeling between the stepbrothers, and his assumed ignorance was so transparent that Mark, had he not been blinded by his self-conceit, might easily have seen through it.

"I suppose," said James, "you will see a little life now that you are your own master and have plenty of money."

"I don't know exactly what you mean, James. There isn't much life to be seen in Bridgeville."

"That is true; but still there is some. Suppose now"—by this time they were in front of the saloon, which, besides a bar, contained a billiard and pool table—"suppose now we go in and have a game of billiards."

"It's against the rules, isn't it?" asked Mark.

"What do you care for the rules?" said James, contemptuously.

"If the old man hears of it, we shall get into hot water."

By the "old man" Mark meant the Rev. Dr. Brush, the venerable and respected principal of the Bridgeville Academy, but such boys as he have very little respect for the constituted authorities.

"Why need he know it? We will slip in when no one is looking. Did you ever play a game of billiards?"

"I never played over half a dozen games in my life."

"You ought to know how to play. It is a splendid game. Come in."

Mark did not make very strong opposition, and the two boys, first looking cautiously in different directions, entered the saloon.

Toward the entrance was the bar, and in the rear of the saloon were two tables.

"Won't you have a drink, Mark?" asked James.

Mark hesitated.

"Oh, come now, it won't hurt. Two glasses of whisky, John."

"All right, Mr. Carson," said the barkeeper, to whom James was well known.

James tossed off his glass with the air of an old drinker, but Mark drank his more slowly.

"There, I know you feel better, Mark."

"Now, John, give me the balls. We'll play a game of billiards."

"All right, sir."

"I'll discount you, Mark," said James, "to give you a fair chance. It is about the same thing as giving you half the game. Or, if you like, I will give you seventeen points to start with, and then you will only have seventeen to make, while I am making thirty-four."

"I like that best."

"Now shall we play for the drinks?"

"We have just had a drink."

"We'll have another."

"Won't that be too much? I don't want to get drunk."

"Two drinks won't do you any harm. Very well. Now let us string for the lead."

There is no need of describing the game in detail. Mark was only a novice, while James could really make three or four points to his one. He restrained himself, however, so that he only beat Mark by two points.

"You did splendidly, Mark," he said. Considering how little you have played, you did remarkably well. Why, you made a run of three."

"Yes, I did pretty well," said Mark, flattered by his companion's praises.

"I had hard work to beat you, I can tell you that. As it was, you came within two points of beating. Don't you like the game?"

"Very much."

"I thought you would. Shall we have another game?"

"I don't mind," answered Mark.

He knew that he ought to be in his room writing a composition to be delivered the next day, but such obligations sat easily upon Mark, and he did not hesitate long.

That time James allowed him to score sixteen, so that Mark was only beaten by one point.

"You see, you are improving," said James. "I played a better game that time than before, and still you came within one of beating me."

"I think I shall become a good player in time," said Mark, complacently.

"Yes, and in a very short time. Now," said James, "I have a proposal to make to you."

"What is it?"

"We'll bet twenty-five cents on the next game, to give a little interest to it."

"Mark had no special scruples against betting, which is only one form of gambling, but he decidedly objected to losing money, so he answered, cautiously:

"I don't know about that. You beat me both of the other games."

"That's true; but you play better now than you did at first."

"That may be so."

"What are twenty-five cents, anyway? I expect to lose it, but it will increase the interest of the game."

So Mark was persuaded, and the game was played.

James Carson managed to let Mark beat him by five shots, and the latter was correspondingly elated.

"You beat me after all," said James, pretending to be much disappointed, "and by five points. I'll tell you what I'll do—I'll give you the same odds, and bet a dollar on the next game. I suppose it's foolish, but I'll risk it!"

"Done!" said Mark, eagerly.

His cupidity was excited, and he felt sure of winning the dollar, as he had the twenty-five cents. But James had no idea of playing off now, and he played a better game, as he was well able to do. The result was that Mark was beaten by three points.

He looked quite crestfallen.

"I had better shows than you," said James. "I couldn't do it once in five times. Will you play again?"

Mark agreed to it with some hesitation, and he was again beaten.

"You had luck against you. Another day you will succeed better. Have you played enough?"

"Yes," answered Mark, annoyed.

He had four games to pay for and two dollars in bets, and it made rather an expensive afternoon.

"Have another drink? I'll treat," said James, who could afford to be liberal.

Mark accepted, and then, flushed and excited, he left the saloon, just as Frank came up, as described in the first part of the chapter. On the whole, he was sorry to meet his step-brother just at this time.

Frank stopped, and his attention was drawn to Mark's flushed face.

CHAPTER XIII.

MARK GETS INTO TROUBLE.

MARK nodded slightly and was about to pass without a word, when Frank said, quietly:

"I am sorry to see you coming out of such a place, Mark."

"What is it to you, anyway?" returned Mark, rudely.

"Not much, perhaps," replied Frank, calmly, "but I don't like to see my acquaintances coming out of a liquor saloon."

"It won't hurt you," said Mark, irritably.

"No, it won't hurt me, but if the principal should hear of it, it would not be pleasant for you. You know students are strictly forbidden to enter any saloon?"

"I suppose you mean to tell of me," said Mark, hastily, and not altogether without uneasiness.

"You are mistaken. I am not a talebearer."

"Then there is no need to say any more about it. Come along, James!"

Frank's interference was well meant, but, as we shall see, it did harm rather than good.

As Mark left the saloon, he had half decided not to enter it again. He was three dollars out of pocket, and this did not suit him at all.

In fact, Mark was rather a mean boy, and it was with considerable reluctance that he had handed over to his companion the two dollars with which to pay for the games.

Moreover, he was mortified at losing the two games of billiards, when so great odds had been given him.

James Carson was no scholar, but he was sharp enough to perceive the state of Mark's feelings, and he also saw how he was affected by Frank's remonstrance.

He decided to take advantage of this, and strengthen his hold on Mark.

"Well, Mark," he said, "I suppose you'll give up playing billiards now."

"Why should I?"

"Because your stepbrother doesn't approve of it. You won't dare to go into the saloon after he has forbidden you," he continued, with a sneer.

"What do you mean, James? Do you suppose I care that"—snapping his fingers—"for what Frank says, or even thinks, either?"

"I didn't know but you might stand in fear of him."

"Do you mean to insult me?" demanded Mark, hotly.

"Insult you! My dear friend, what can you be thinking of? Why, I like you ten times as much as that muff, Frank Courtney."

"Then what did you mean by what you said?" asked Mark, more calmly.

"I will tell you. I got an idea, from what Frank said once, that he was in charge of you—well, not exactly that, but that he looked after you."

This was a wicked falsehood, as Frank had never intimated any such thing. In fact, he had generally kept quite aloof from James.

Mark, however, fell into the trap, and never thought of doubting what his companion said.

"If Frank said that, I've a great mind to whip him," said Mark, angrily.

"Oh, I wouldn't notice him, if I were you!" said James. "For my part, I didn't believe what he said. I felt sure that a fine, spirited boy like you wouldn't submit to his dictation."

"I should say not—the impudent fellow!"

"When he spoke to you just now," continued James, "one would really have thought he was your uncle, or guardian, and that you were a little boy."

"I'll show him what I think of him and his advice. I hadn't thought of going to the saloon to-morrow, but now I will."

"Bravo! I like your spirit!" said James, admiringly. It is just the way to treat him. Shall I come round with you about the same hour as to-day?"

"Yes, I wish you would."

When the two boys parted company, James Carson smiled to himself.

"What a fool Mark is!" he thought. "He thinks he is his own master, but I am going to twist him round my little finger. He's a sweet youth, but he's got money, and I mean to have some of it. Why, he tells me his father allows him eight dollars a week for spending money. If I manage well, I can get more than half away from him in bets."

The next day James called for Mark, as agreed upon, and again the two boys went to the billiard saloon. The performance of the day before was repeated.

James Carson, while flattering Mark's poor play, managed to beat in every game but one on which money was staked, and came out the richer by a dollar and a half.

"I am very unlucky," grumbled Mark, in a tone of dissatisfaction.

"So you were, Mark," admitted his sympathizing friend. "You made some capital shots, though, and if I hadn't been so lucky, you would have come out the victor in every game."

"But I didn't."

"No, you didn't; but you can't have such beastly luck all the time."

"I guess I'd better give up billiards. In two days I have spent five dollars. It doesn't pay."

"No doubt Frank will be gratified when he hears that you have given up playing. He will think it is because you are afraid of him."

James had touched the right cord, and poor Mark was once more in his toils.

"It's lucky for me that Frank spoke to him," thought James. "It makes it much easier for me to manage him."

One thing, however, James had not taken

into account. There were others besides Frank who were liable to interfere with his management, and who had the authority to make their interference effectual.

On the day succeeding, as James and Mark were in the campus, Herbert Grant approached them.

Now Herbert was the janitor of the academy. He also was employed by the principal to summon students who had incurred censure to his study, where they received a suitable reprimand.

It was not a pleasant duty, but some one must do it, and Herbert always discharged it in a gentlemanly manner, which could not, or ought not, to offend the school-fellows who were unlucky enough to receive a summons.

"Boys," said he, "I am sorry to be the bearer of unpleasant news, but Dr. Brush would like to see you in his study."

"Both of us?" asked James.

"Yes."

"Are there any others summoned?"

"No."

Mark and his companion looked at each other with perturbed glances. No one cared to visit the principal on such an errand. Corporal punishment was never resorted to in the Bridgeville Academy, but the doctor's dignified rebuke was dreaded more than blows would have been from some men.

"What do you think it is, James?" said Mark, uneasily.

"I think it's the saloon," answered James, in a low voice.

"But how could he have found it out? No one saw us go in or come out."

The billiard saloon was at some distance from the academy building, and for that reason the two boys had felt more secure in visiting it.

"I'll tell you how it came out," said James, suddenly.

"How?" asked Mark.

"You remember Frank saw us coming out day before yesterday."

"He said he wouldn't tell."

"I know he said so, but it was too good an opportunity for him to gratify his spite against you. You may depend upon it, Mark, that we are indebted for this little favor to your kind stepbrother."

It was not very difficult for Mark to believe anything against Frank, and he instantly adopted his companion's idea.

"The mean sneak!" he said. "I'll come up with him! I'll tell my father not to give him any money for the next month. I'll—I'll get him to apprentice Frank to a shoemaker! Perhaps then he won't put on so many airs."

"Good for you! I admire your pluck!" said James, slapping Mark on the back. "You are true grit, you are! Just teach the fellow a lesson."

"See if I don't!"

Mark nodded his head resolutely, and went into the presence of Dr. Brush, thirsting for vengeance against his stepbrother, who, he felt persuaded, had informed against him.

If Frank had known his suspicions he would have been very much surprised. As it happened, however, he did not even know that his stepbrother had been summoned to the doctor's study. Had he met Herbert, the latter would have told him; but after receiving his list, it so chanced that he and his friend did not meet.

The fact was that a young man employed as tutor in mathematics in the academy, while taking an afternoon walk, had seen Mark and James Carson leaving the liquor saloon, and, as in duty bound, had reported the same to the principal.

Mr. Triangle, however, had not been observed by either of the two boys, and therefore they were led off on a false scent.

"What do you think the old man will say?" asked Mark, uneasily, as they ascended the stairs to the principal's study.

"He'll give us a raking down, I suppose," said James. "He will come down heavy on us."

"I wish I were out of it."

"Oh, it's not worthy minding! We haven't committed murder, have we? What's the harm in a game of billiards?"

"Not much, perhaps; but the drinking and betting are certainly objectionable."

The boys knocked at the door, and the full, deep voice of Dr. Brush was heard to say: "Come in!"

CHAPTER XIV.

SUSPENDED.

DR. BRUSH was seated at a table covered with papers, in a large armchair. He was an elderly man of dignified presence, not a petty tyrant such as is sometimes found in a similar position, but a man who commanded respect without an effort.

Mark Manning and James Carson entered his presence a little nervously.

"Young gentlemen," said the doctor, gravely, "I am informed that you have violated one of the rules of the academy by frequenting a billiard saloon where liquor is sold."

"Who told you, sir?" asked Mark.

"That is not to the purpose," said the principal, gravely.

"But I should like to know who informed on me," persisted Mark.

"Whoever did so acted as your true friend, Manning; but there is no occasion for you to know who it was. Is it true?"

Mark would have been glad to deny the charge, and would not have felt any scruples about doing so, if it would have done any good.

But it was clear, even to him, that he would not be believed, and that denial would only make his position worse. So he made a virtue of necessity, and answered:

"I have been in once or twice, sir."

"Exactly how many times have you been to the saloon?"

"Three times."

"What did you do there?"

"We played billiards."

"Did you order anything at the bar?"

"Yes, sir," said Mark, reluctantly.

"Carson, you accompanied Manning, did you not?" said Dr. Brush, turning to Mark's companion.

"Yes, sir."

"And I suppose you also played billiards and drank?"

"Well, yes, sir, I believe I did."

"You were aware, were you not, that it was against the regulations of the school?"

"I suppose it must have slipped my mind," answered James, trying to look as innocent as possible.

Dr. Brush frowned, for he saw clearly that this was but a subterfuge.

"If this were true," he continued, "it would be no excuse. As students, it is your duty to make yourselves acquainted with the rules that govern the institution. In point of fact, I cannot believe that either of you is ignorant of the rule forbidding students to frequent places where liquor is sold. It is hardly necessary for me to defend the propriety of the rule. Intemperance is a fruitful source of vice and crime, and I cannot allow the youth under my charge to form habits of indulgence which may blast all their prospects, and lead to the most ruinous consequences."

"We didn't drink much," said Mark.

"I shall not inquire how much you drank. In drinking a single glass, you violated the rule of the school, and I cannot pass over it."

"What is he going to do with us, I wonder?" thought Mark.

He was not required to wonder long.

"As this is your first offense, so far as I know," proceeded the principal, "I will not be severe. You are both suspended from the institution for the remainder of the term, and are required to leave Bridgeville by the early train to-morrow morning for your respective homes. I shall write to your parents, explaining the cause of your suspension."

But a week remained of the term, and the punishment was mild, but both boys were mortified and left the study crestfallen.

Mark was the first to recover his spirits.

"It is not so bad, James," he said. "To-morrow will be Saturday, and I should go home, anyway. I don't mind staying at home next week."

"What will your father say?"

"Oh, I'll make it all right with him! I

don't mind much what he says. I guess he got into scrapes himself when he was a boy."

"My father isn't so easily managed. Just as likely as not, he'll cut off my allowance for a month; and that'll be no joke!"

"My father won't do that," said Mark. "If he did, I would raise a fuss."

"Would that do any good?"

"I'll bet it would!"

"Mark, you are a true friend of mine, aren't you?" asked James.

"Yes," said Mark, but not very warmly.

"Of course, I know you are, and you will do me a favor, won't you?"

"What is it?" asked Mark, cautiously.

"Lend me five dollars till the beginning of next term."

"I haven't got the money, Carson. You know how much I have lost in the last two or three days. "I've hardly got money enough to take me home."

"Can't you borrow it of Frank for me?"

"Ask him yourself. I am not going to ask a favor of the boy who reported me."

"You'll have money when you get home, won't you?"

"I suppose so."

"Then just send me a five-dollar bill in a letter. The old man will cut off my allowance during vacation, and it will do me no end of good."

If he had known Mark a little better, he

would have spared himself the trouble of asking a loan.

"You must excuse me," said Mark, coldly. "I am saving my money for a particular purpose, and can't spare five dollars."

"I would pay you back at the beginning of the term."

"No, I can't do it," said Mark, looking annoyed. "Stay! There is Frank, just across the campus. I am going over to charge him with betraying us."

Frank, who was quite ignorant of Mark's trouble, was surprised when the latter approached him with a frown and said, harshly:

"You won't make anything by what you have done, Frank Courtney!"

"Will you be kind enough to tell me what I have done?" asked Frank, calmly.

"You've been to Dr. Brush and told him about our playing billiards."

"You are entirely mistaken, Mark. I did not suppose he knew."

"It must have been you. He told us some one had informed him, and you were the only one who knew. It's a mean trick, isn't it, Carson?"

"Awfully mean!"

"I have already told you that the information did not come from me. It may be the best thing for you that it has been found out, for it was doing you no good to frequent such places."

"I don't want to hear any of your preaching, Frank Courtney. I guess I can manage my own affairs without any advice from you."

"I don't care to intrude any advice," said Frank. "I have not much reason to feel interested in you."

"You'd better look out how you treat me, though," said Mark, insolently. "I know very well you dislike me, but it won't be safe for you to show it while you are a dependent on my father."

"I don't propose to be a dependent on him long," said Frank, quietly. "The truth of it is, you and your father are dependent upon property which of right belongs to me. The time may come when I shall be able to show this."

"What does he mean?" thought Mark, uneasily. "Will he contest the will?"

It was perhaps an evidence of Mark's shrewdness that he had some doubts about the validity of the will under which his father inherited.

It was possible that his stepmother might have made the will through the influence of her husband; but, devoted as she was to Frank, and generally a clear-sighted woman in matters of business, it did not seem very probable.

"There's been some trickery," thought Mark, "and my father knows what it is. However, that's his affair, not mine, and I am glad that he has got the property. I shall fare better, at any rate, and if there's any fuss made, they can't say anything against me."

It was important that Frank should be prevented from doing anything that might lead to an investigation which might develop facts better left in secret.

Mark did not reply to Frank's last words, but walked away with James Carson.

The latter, however, soon made an excuse for leaving Mark, from whom he had no more to hope, and he went back to find Frank.

Our hero regarded him with some surprise, and waited for him to speak.

With an assumption of frankness, Carson said:

"I want to tell you, Frank, that I don't believe with Mark that you informed against us."

"You do no more than justice," said Frank.

"Of course you know that Mark is prejudiced against you."

"I suppose he is."

"And that makes him ready to suspect you of anything. Dr. Brush has suspended us for the remainder of the term."

"I am sorry to hear it."

"Oh, it won't matter much! It's only a week, you know. But there is one little inconvenience to me. I have spent so much money lately that I have hardly funds enough to carry me home."

Frank didn't like James Carson, but he was of a generous and helpful disposition.

"Can I be of any service to you?" he asked.

"If you could lend me five dollars till the beginning of next term, it would be a great help."

Frank drew a five-dollar bill from his pocket-book, and handed it to James.

"Thank you," said the latter, joyfully. "I'll be sure to return it."

"I didn't think it would be so easy," he chuckled, as he walked away. "With the ten dollars in my purse, part of it won from Mark, and this money, I am in funds. Mark's a mean fellow. I wish I could have made more out of him."

CHAPTER XV.

MR. MANNING'S NEW PLAN.

Mark so represented his school difficulty to his father that he incurred but slight censure.

Indeed, Mr. Manning was so absorbed in plans for getting the greatest enjoyment out of the estate of which he had obtained possession by doubtful means that he didn't care to be disturbed about such a trifle as his son's suspension.

He felt more disposed to blame Frank, whom Mark charged with betraying him.

"What does Frank say about it?" asked Mr. Manning.

"Of course he denies it," said Mark, "but it can't be any one else."

"He is acting very unwisely," said Mr. Manning, compressing his thin lips.

"So I told him, but he said he didn't mean to be a dependent on you long."

"How is he going to avoid it?"

"I don't know."

"I have had some intimation from Col. Vincent, who appears to be in his confidence. He wants to leave us."

"To go away?"

"Yes."

"But you won't let him?"

"I have been thinking about that, Mark, and I may give my permission. The fact is, he stands in the way of some plans I have formed. I am thinking of traveling."

"Not without me?" said Mark, hastily.

"No; you shall go with me, but I don't care to take Frank."

"You might leave him at school."

"I might, but how do I know that he might not hatch some mischief while we are gone?"

"He might make some fuss about the property," suggested Mark.

"Has he hinted anything of that kind to you?" asked his father, quickly.

"Yes. Only yesterday he said that the property belonged by right to him."

Mr. Manning looked thoughtful, and watched Mark narrowly to see if from his manner he could divine the boy's intentions.

Later that same evening, Mark having retired early in consequence of a headache, Frank found himself alone with his stepfather, and took advantage of the opportunity to speak of the plan he had formed.

"Mr. Manning," he said, "if you are at leisure, I should like to speak with you a few minutes."

"Proceed," said his stepfather, waving his hand.

"But a week remains of the school term. Did you propose that I should return there at the end of the vacation?"

"Humph! I had not thought much on the subject."

"It has all along been intended that I should go to college when prepared, but I don't think I care much about it."

"In that case," said his stepfather, with alacrity, "you would only be throwing away time and money by going."

He was quite ready to agree to Frank's surrender of the college plan for two reasons.

A college course would be expensive. Again, should he turn his attention to the law, he might hereafter give him trouble about the estate.

"I don't think I should throw away my time, for, if I went to college, I should go there to work faithfully; but I have a fancy for a more stirring life."

"It might be a good plan for you to learn a trade," said Mr. Manning, reflectively.

"Learn a trade!" exclaimed Frank, in surprise.

"Yes; it would always enable you to earn a living."

"Do you intend Mark to learn a trade?" asked Frank, quickly.

"No; his case is very different from yours."

"Why is it different?"

"It is not necessary for me to explain," answered his stepfather, stiffly.

"If there were any need of it, Mr. Manning, I would not object to learn a trade," said Frank. "I have no false pride on the subject. But my tastes are more for mercantile business."

"I may be able to find you a place somewhere. I have a friend in the dry-goods business, who would receive you at my recommendation."

"Thank you!" said Frank, hastily. "But if you will allow me, I would prefer to look around for myself."

"What is it you want, then?"

"Your permission to go out into the world, and try to make a living."

"And if you don't," said Mr. Manning, "I suppose you expect me to defray your expenses?"

"If I did have such an expectation, I think I should be justified, in view of the large property which my mother left," said Frank, pointedly.

"She left it to me," said his stepfather.

"So it appears, at any rate. But I shall not call upon you to pay my board. Give me your permission to go where I please, with a small sum of money to start me, and I shall be satisfied."

"And what will the world say? That I, your stepfather, to whom you have a right to look for maintenance, had driven you out to earn your own living! It would be unjust, of course, but the world is ever unjust."

And Mr. Manning assumed a look of wronged innocence, which would have imposed on any one who knew him but slightly.

"I shall defend you from any such charge," said Frank. "I shall say that you were only yielding to my request."

"I will think of it, my dear boy," said Mr. Manning, graciously. "I already feel inclined to grant it, because it is your request. I shall be sorry to be separated from you; but I am willing to sacrifice my own feelings, if it will give you pleasure."

This did not impose upon Frank, who had a correct idea of the degree of fondness which Mr. Manning had for his society, but he was too well satisfied with the prospect of obtaining the permission he desired to imply any doubts.

"Again," continued his stepfather, "Whatever you may say to the contrary, I know that the world will censure me; but I shall have the approval of my own conscience, and with that I can defy the world."

Mr. Manning certainly did look like a righteous man when he said this, and he beamed upon his stepson with a glance that was actually affectionate.

"Go back to school," he said, "and when you return I shall be able to give you a definite answer."

Indeed, nothing could have suited Mr. Manning's plans better. He would get rid of the care and nearly the whole expense of his obnoxious stepson, while with his son Mark he would be spending the revenues of the estate which belonged to Frank.

During the coming week he arranged his plans for a prolonged absence from the Cedars. He wrote to New York to engage passage on a steamer bound for Liverpool, and quietly waited for the end of Frank's school term to release him from a care which had grown burdensome.

Frank returned to the Bridgeville Academy without Mark. As may be supposed, however, he did not feel the loss of his society.

He at once communicated to his chosen friend, Herbert Grant, his probable departure from school.

"I am sorry to hear it, Frank," said Herbert, soberly. "Do you think you are acting wisely?"

"I am not acting as I would have done had

my mother lived," answered Frank; "but you must remember that my position in life has very much changed. I am a poor boy."

"Hardly that, when there is so much property in the family."

"I know Mr. Manning too well to believe that I shall derive much benefit from it. No, Herbert, I have my own living to make, and I want to make it in my own way."

"It is a sad change for you, Frank."

"No, I can't say that. I don't know how it is, Herbert, but I am rather glad to have all this thrown upon me. I enjoy feeling that I have got to work."

"I have a chance of enjoying the same feelings," said Herbert, with a smile.

"I wish we could start together, Herbert. Couldn't you go with me?"

Herbert shook his head.

"Father has a plan for me," he said. "I am to learn his trade, and shall commence next week. I don't particularly like it, but it is well to have a trade to fall back upon."

"Mr. Manning wanted me to learn a trade."

"There is no occasion for your doing so."

"I don't know about that. If I had a particular fancy for any, I wouldn't mind choosing it, but I am better suited for something else."

"What is your plan? What will you do first?"

"My father has a cousin in the city of Newark, New Jersey, only a few miles from New York. Four years ago, he and his family made us a visit, and he was urgent then that we should return the visit. I will, first of all, go to him, and ask his advice. He is a business man, and he may be able to put me in the way of obtaining a position."

"I think you will succeed, Frank, but it will be harder than you think for. You don't know what poverty is yet. I have never known anything else."

"If you do succeed, Herbert, I may be able to find something for you."

"I wish you might," Herbert replied; but he was not as sanguine as Frank.

He understood, better than his friend, that for a boy to set out alone into the great world to earn a living is a serious undertaking.

CHAPTER XVI.

GOOD-BY.

Frank had fixed upon the Tuesday morning succeeding the close of the academic term for his departure from home. Monday was devoted to a few necessary preparations and a few calls on old friends, among them Col. Vincent, the owner of Ajax.

"My dear Frank," said the colonel, kindly, "I feel a strong interest in your welfare, more especially because of the wrong which I do not scruple to say has been done you. What does Mr. Manning say to your plan?"

"He makes no objection," said Frank.

"Suppose he had done so?"

"I would not have run away. He is my stepfather and guardian, and I would have endured staying at home as well as I could."

"There you are right, Frank. Though I have a poor opinion of Mr. Manning, he is not likely to treat you in a manner to justify your going away without his permission. From what I have heard within the last week, I suspect that he feels relieved to have you go."

"What have you heard, sir?"

"That Mr. Manning will shortly sail for Europe, taking Mark with him."

Frank was surprised, having no suspicion of this.

"Now are you not sorry that you have decided to go out into the world to earn a living when you might have seen something of the Old World?"

"Mr. Manning would never have taken me along," answered Frank, quietly, "nor should I have enjoyed traveling with him and Mark."

"Of the two, who would interfere the more with your enjoyment?"

"Mark."

"Then you prefer the father to the son?" said the colonel.

"The father has much more agreeable manners. I don't think Mark could be agreeable if he tried."

Col. Vincent smiled.

"Perhaps you are right, Frank," he said. "Now, as your father's old friend, I shall exact a promise from you."

"What is it, sir?"

"You are going out into the world to earn your own living. Boys of your age are apt to think it an easy thing. I have seen more of life, and I am sure you will find it more difficult than you suppose. You may find yourself in difficulty, possibly in want. In that case, promise to let me know, and I will come to your assistance."

"I will, sir," answered Frank.

Though he gave this promise, he was more than half inclined to question the truth of Col. Vincent's remarks as to the difficulty of earning a living. He was full of confidence, as most boys are, the result of his inexperience. To be sure, his scheme was not as Quixotic as that of some boys, who leave good homes, armed with revolvers, to hunt for Indians. If a real Indian, in his war paint, should suddenly make his appearanee, he would put to flight a hundred of boy hunters.

I wish it understood, therefore, that though Frank had the permission of his guardian to leave home, and though he was better fitted than the great majority of boys to make his way in the world, I agree with Col. Vincent in considering his plan a doubtful one, requiring for success not only pluck and persistency, but good health and good luck. Not many boys can expect an uninterrupted course of prosperity when thrown upon their own exertions.

The time came for Frank to say good-by to Mr. Manning and Mark, and the house which had been his home from infancy.

His stepfather handed him a small pocket-book.

"Frank," he said, "in this pocket-book you will find twenty-five dollars. It is not much, but——"

"I am satisfied, sir," said Frank. "It won't be long before I am earning something."

"I hope your anticipations may be realized, but it is possible that you may require help."

"I think not, sir."

"I will authorize my banker to pay you the same sum—twenty-five dollars—every three months. Of course, it is not enough to support you; but, as you say it is your intention to procure a place——"

"Yes, sir."

"It will probably be enough to make up any deficiency that may exist in your income. I am aware that you do not regard me as—as I would like to have you; but I am resigned to be misunderstood, and I merely call your attention to the fact that I have given you my free permission to carry out your own plans and have given you more assistance than you asked for."

"That's true, sir."

"Should any one in your hearing condemn me for what I have done, I depend upon your defending me."

"I will state the facts, sir. I will take the entire responsibility for anything that may result from the step I have taken."

Mr. Manning looked well pleased. Things were taking the course he desired, and for the paltry sum of one hundred dollars a year, he was getting rid of an obnoxious stepson, while appearing to confer a favor upon him.

He was even enlisting the boy as his advocate and defender against any attacks or criticism from the world.

"I will give you the name of my banker in New York," Mr. Manning proceeded. "At the end of each quarter you may apply to him for the sum I have mentioned. I may—it is not quite decided—I may make a journey with Mark. I find that my health has been affected by the great trial I have met with in the loss of my lamented wife, and the anxiety I have naturally suffered on her account."

As Mr. Manning was looking unusually well, his attempt to look weak and suffering was a failure, and Frank kept silent, being unable to express a sympathy he did not feel.

"If," said Mr. Manning, doubtfully, "you would like to give up your plan and travel with us, I think it can be arranged. You would be company for Mark."

Frank could not help glancing at Mark, to see how far his appearance bore out his father's statement.

He was not surprised to observe that his stepbrother's brow was overcast and that he looked angrily at his father, alarmed lest the offer should be accepted.

"Thank you, Mr. Manning," said Frank; "but at present I should prefer to go out in the world and see what I can do for myself. Some day I hope to travel; but I am young and can wait."

Mark looked very much relieved at this decision. Judging Frank by himself, he feared that it would be accepted, and he could not help deciding in his own mind that Frank was a fool to prefer work to a pleasant journey.

He was satisfied that his father never would have taken Frank, even had the latter decided to accept the proposal, but it would have occasioned delay, and Mark was impatient to get started on his journey.

The Cedars he regarded as a stupid place, and he was eager to visit the cities of Europe, where he could find plenty of amusement.

"Perhaps you are right, Frank," said his stepfather, disguising the satisfaction he felt. "If, however, you should find that you have made a mistake, you will do me the justice to remember that I gave you your choice."

Knowing, as he did, that the offer was not genuine, Frank remained silent. He could not make up his mind to express gratitude, and therefore said nothing.

Here the carriage drove up to the door to convey Frank to the railway station. Mindful of appearances, Mr. Manning accompanied him to the cars, and in presence of several neighbors bade him an effusively affectionate farewell.

So Frank was fairly started on his campaign.

CHAPTER XVII.

ERASTUS TARBOX, OF NEWARK.

ERASTUS TARBOX kept a dry-goods store in the city of Newark, New Jersey. He was well-to-do, not so much because of his enterprise and skill as a merchant as because of his extreme poverty. Some people called it parsimoney. He only employed two clerks to assist him in his store, and they, as well as the boy who carried out the parcels and ran the errands, were paid scarcely more than two-thirds the rates paid in neighboring stores.

To some it may seem strange that Mr. Tarbox was able to obtain assistants at such low rates, but those who know how many dry-goods clerks there always are seeking employment will not need to wonder.

Neither will it be a matter of surprise that when Mr. Tarbox chanced to secure a superior clerk he was not able to keep him long, for, at the first hint of higher wages, the employer exhibited such dissatisfaction that the salesman was very apt to throw up his situation in disgust.

Mr. Tarbox prided himself upon his relationship to the Courtneys. They were rich, and riches, in his eyes, were a great merit. He often sighed to think that there was no chance for him to benefit by a share of the large property owned by his cousins. Without hope of personal advantage, however, he had always been obsequious to them, and often took occasion to mention them, by way of enhancing his own social credit somewhat.

Mr. Tarbox had heard of Mrs. Courtney's death, but had not heard the particulars of the will. He took it for granted that Frank was sole heir, and it did cross his mind more than once how very agreeable it would be if he could be selected as guardian of the rich young heir. Of course, he knew that there was no probability of it, since the stepfather would undoubtedly be appointed to that position.

Mr. Tarbox had just sold a calico dress pattern to a poor woman, when his attention was drawn to the entrance of Frank Courtney, who entered the store, valise in hand.

Mr. Tarbox was rather short-sighted, and did not immediately recognize the son of his rich cousin.

"What can I do for you, young man?" he asked, in his business tone.

"This is Mr. Tarbox, I believe?" said Frank, who did not know his relatives very well.

"Yes, that is my name."

"I am Frank Courtney."

"Bless my soul!" ejaculated Mr. Tarbox, surprized and delighted. "When did you arrive in Newark?"

"I have only just arrived."

"I do hope you are going to make us a visit," said Mr. Tarbox, cordially.

"Thank you!" answered Frank, cheered by this warm reception. "If you are sure it won't inconvenience you."

"Inconvenience me! We shall be delighted to have you with us."

"I wish," thought he, "that Frank would be contented to board with me. He can afford to pay a handsome price, and there would be a good deal of profit to be made. I must try to make it pleasant for him."

"You are very kind to think of us, my dear young relative," continued Mr. Tarbox, rubbing his hands in high good humor. "Accept my warmest sympathy in your great affliction. I was deeply grieved to hear of your dear mother's death."

Mr. Tarbox was a remarkably plain man. He had a mottled face, watery eyes, and a long, thin, tapering nose, and a low forehead, partially covered with iron-gray hair. Still he was a relation, and Frank's heart warmed to him when he spoke so feelingly of the mother whom he so much missed.

"You must come up and see Mrs. Tarbox. She will be delighted to see you."

Mr. Tarbox lived over his store. There was a door from the street adjoining the shop front. Mr. Tarbox opened it with a pass-key, and conducted Frank upstairs, ushering him into a gloomy parlor, with stiff, straight-backed chairs, ranged at regular intervals along the sides of the room, and a marble-topped center table, with two or three books lying upon it. There was a framed engraving, representing Washington crossing the Delaware, over the mantel, and two plaster figures and similar ornaments on the mantelpiece. The whole aspect of the room chilled Frank.

"Wait here, and I will call my wife," said Mr. Tarbox.

Frank sat down on a hard sofa and awaited the entrance of Mrs. Tarbox.

She came in, a tall, thin woman, about as handsome for a woman as her husband was for a man. Indeed, they were very well matched. She was quite as mean as he, and between them they managed to make annually a sensible addition to their worldly possessions.

Mr. Tarbox privately hinted his hopes respecting Frank to his wife, and she instantly agreed that it would be a most eligible arrangement.

"We must make him contented, my dear,"

said her husband. "Give him the best bedroom, and I think it might be well to have something a little extra for supper."

"I did intend to put on the rest of that cold mutton," said Mrs. Tarbox, doubtfully.

"It won't do, Martha. There is only a little of it, you know, and the boy has been traveling, and, of course, is hungry. What do you say, now, to some nice beefsteak?"

"Beefsteak is high now," said Mrs. Tarbox. "Still, if we buy round steak—that is cheaper than sirloin or tenderloin."

"And quite as good," said her economical partner. "We can tell Frank, however, that no sirloin was to be had so late in the day at the markets."

Mrs. Tarbox nodded her head, approving the suggestion.

This little matter being adjusted, the husband and wife entered the parlor where our hero was waiting patiently.

"This is our young cousin, Martha," said Mr. Tarbox, smiling pleasantly.

"Welcome to Newark," said Mrs. Tarbox, extending her hand. "And how did you leave your stepfather?"

"He is well," said Frank, coolly.

The two exchanged glances. It was clear that Frank did not like his stepfather, and this was satisfactory to them. There was the more chance of his leaving him and boarding with them.

"The children will be so glad to see you," said Mr. Tarbox; "won't they, Martha?"

"Delighted!" assured the lady.

"Pliny must be about your age. How old are you, by the way?"

"Sixteen."

"Just Pliny's age. Do you remember him?"

Frank remembered a tall, thin stripling who had accompanied his parents to the Cedars, and who appeared to have an inexhaustible appetite.

"Yes, I remember him. Does he go to school?"

"No; Pliny is in a store," answered Mr. Tarbox.

"Your store?"

"Oh, no! I thought it would be better for him to enter the employ of a stranger. He is in a bookstore."

There was one great advantage in Pliny's entering the employ of a stranger. He was paid four dollars a week, whereas Mr. Tarbox paid his boy but two. Here, then, was a clear gain of two dollars a week.

"But you must be tired," said Mrs. Tarbox. "You will see the children at supper. Martha, I think Frank would like to go to his room."

The best bedroom was over the parlor. It was rather more cheerful, because lighter.

"Here," said Mr. Tarbox, "you must make yourself at home. Martha, isn't one of the drawers in that bureau empty? I thought so. Take your clothes out of the valise and put them away. Now, is there anything you would like?"

"Only a little water to wash in," said Frank. "You are both very kind."

"We hope to make you comfortable. You are our relative, you know."

The water was brought up by Mrs. Tarbox herself, and Frank was left alone, on the whole well pleased with his reception.

CHAPTER XVIII.

AN UNPLEASANT DISCOVERY.

It never occurred to Frank that his cordial reception was wholly due to his supposed wealth. Had he known the Tarbox family better, he would have had no uncertainty on this point. As it was the discovery was soon made.

It was not long before the supper-bell rang, and Frank descended the stairs, guided by Mr. Tarbox himself. There our hero saw the younger branches of the family—Pliny, a thin, lanky youth, with pale-brown hair plastered to the sides of his head with bear's grease, and Julia, who was a smaller edition of her mother. There were two children still younger, who do not need describing.

"All my olive branches are before you, my dear young cousin," said Mr. Tarbox, waving his hand. "A peaceful, happy family. Children, this is our esteemed relative, Frank Courtney. You remember visiting his delightful home, the Cedars."

"Yes, pa," said Julia.

Pliny said nothing, but stared at Frank, inwardly considering whether it would be possible to borrow some money of him.

Frank looked around him, and tried to believe that he should like his young cousins; but they did not look at all attractive. But he wished to be polite, and said:

"I am glad to meet you all. I hope we shall become better acquainted."

"No doubt you will," said Mr. Tarbox. "They are rather bashful, but they long to know you."

"How are you?" said Pliny, in a sudden burst of sociability.

"Pretty well, thank you!" answered Frank, finding it rather difficult to preserve his gravity.

"I am in a store," said Pliny.

"In your father's store?"

"No. He wouldn't pay me as much as I get where I am."

Mr. Tarbox looked embarrassed.

"A smaller boy answered my purpose," he said, in an explanatory manner. "Pliny is suited for higher duties. But our supper is ready. It is frugal compared with yours at the Cedars, my dear Frank, but you are heartily welcome to it."

"It looks very nice, Mr. Tarbox," said our hero, "and I have not been accustomed to luxurious living."

This answer pleased Mr. and Mrs. Tarbox. Even if Frank should become a boarder on liberal terms, they didn't wish to spend too much on their table.

"We couldn't get sirloin steak," said Mr. Tarbox; "but I hope you will find this good."

"No doubt I shall," said Frank, politely.

"You never do buy sirloin steak, ma," said one of the younger darlings.

Mrs. Tarbox frowned.

"Hush, Amelia!" she said. "Little girls should been seen and not heard."

"Do you have to go back to the store, Pliny?" asked Frank.

"Yes; I have to stay till eight o'clock."

"Do you like it?"

"Yes, pretty well; but I like the pay better," chuckled Pliny, who was under the impression that he had said something witty.

"Candid boy!" exclaimed his father, admiringly.

"They pay me four dollars a week," continued Pliny; "but I guess they'll raise me to five in a few months."

"Four dollars a week!" thought Frank. "That isn't much. I am afraid I couldn't live on it."

"Have you been in the place long?" he asked.

"Three months."

"Is that the price usually paid to boys?" inquired Frank.

"Pa only pays his boy two dollars a week," said Amelia.

Here it was Mr. Tarbox's turn to frown.

"The duties of my boy are very simple," he felt obliged to explain.

Frank, knowing Mr. Tarbox to be in business before coming to Newark, had a vague idea of finding a place in his store, but this revelation convinced him that it would be necessary for him to look elsewhere. Even if there had been a vacancy, it was quite out of the question to accept two dollars a week.

"Won't you have another piece of steak?" asked Mrs. Tarbox.

Frank saw that there was but a small piece left, and, though his appetite was not wholly satisfied, he answered:

"No, thank you."

"I will!" said Pliny, quickly.

Mrs. Tarbox frowned at her son, but did not venture to refuse in the presence of her guest. She cut off a small portion of the steak, and, with a severe look, put it on the extended plate of Pliny.

"You've got a good appetite, Pliny," said Julia.

"So would you have, if you had to work like me!" grumbled Pliny.

After the steak came an apple pie, which

was cut into seven pieces. Mrs. Tarbox managed to make Frank's piece a little larger than the rest.

Her husband observed it with approval. He was very desirous that Frank should be satisfied with his fare.

When Pliny rose from the table, saying that he must be getting back to the store, Frank rose also.

"I will go with you," he said, "if you have no objection. I would like to take a walk."

"Come along," said Pliny. "I should like to have company."

"You will be a great deal of company for Pliny," observed Mr. Tarbox, rubbing his hands with satisfaction. "Just of an age and of congenial tastes."

Frank hardly expected to find Pliny very congenial, but he wished to obtain some information, which he thought the latter could give him, and he also wanted to see something of Newark.

"I say, your name is Frank, isn't it?" commenced Pliny.

"Yes."

"The old man's awful glad to see you."

"I am glad of it. He has received me very kindly."

"Got up an extra supper for you. We don't often get steak for supper."

This was rather an embarrassing revelation, and surprised Frank somewhat. The supper had not seemed to him at all extra. It would do, but was far from luxurious.

"I hope you'll stay with us a good while," continued Pliny.

"Thank you."

"You see we shall live better while you are with us, and the rest of us will be gainers."

"I don't want to put your father to any unusual expense."

Oh, he can afford it! But he's stingy, father is. He doesn't spend any more than he can help."

"It is best to be economical, I suppose."

"When you don't carry it too far. I say, Frank," continued Pliny, lowering his voice, "you can't lend me five dollars, can you?"

Frank regarded Pliny with astonishment. The proposal was very abrupt, especially when the shortness of their acquaintance was considered.

"Are you particularly in need of money?" asked Frank.

"Well, you see," said Pliny, "I want it for a particular purpose."

"Why not ask your father for it?"

"Oh, he'd never let me have it!"

Now, in Frank's present circumstances, five dollars represented a good deal of money. He was the more impressed with the necessity of economy since he had found out how small were the wages paid in stores to boys of his age.

He did not feel at all inclined to grant Pliny's request, especially as he had a strong suspicion that it would be a long time before the sum would be returned.

"Why do you apply to me, Pliny?" he asked, seriously.

"Because you have plenty of money. Five dollars would be nothing to you."

"What makes you think I have plenty of money?"

"Didn't your mother die and leave you a big property? Father says you must be worth more than a hundred thousand dollars."

"Your father probably has not heard of the will," said Frank, quietly.

"What was there in the will?" asked Pliny.

"The whole property was left to Mr. Manning."

"Who is he?"

"My stepfather."

"And nothing to you?"

"Nothing to me."

"But he's got to take care of you, hasn't he?"

"It was expected, but I am going to earn my own living, if I can."

Pliny stopped short in blank amazement and whistled.

"Then you haven't got a lot of money?"

"No."

"Won't your stepfather give you part of the property?"

"I haven't asked him, but I don't think he will."

"And why did you come to Newark?'

"I thought your father might give me some help about getting a place."

"If this isn't the richest joke!" said Pliny, laughing uproariously.

"Where is the joke? I don't see it," returned Frank, inclined to be angry.

"The way you have taken in the old man. He thinks you are rich, and has treated you accordingly—got up an extra supper and all that. Oh, it's too good!"

"I certainly didn't intend to take him in, as you call it," said Frank. "The sooner you tell him the better."

"I'll tell him," said Pliny. "I shall enjoy seeing how provoked he'll be."

"I think I will leave you," said Frank, shortly. "I will take a walk by myself."

"Well, don't lose your way. Oh, I wish the store was shut! I want to tell the old man."

And Pliny laughed again, while our hero walked off in disgust.

CHAPTER XIX.

THE WAY OF THE WORLD.

FRANK felt like an impostor when he discovered that his cordial reception was wholly owing to the belief that he was his mother's heir. The situation was unpleasant, and he was impatient to have Mr. Tarbox undeceived. He was sure that Pliny would lose no time in revealing his true position, and decided not to return to the house of Mr. Tarbox till nine o'clock, when the story would have been told.

He wandered about aimlessly till he heard the city clocks strike nine, and then rang the bell at his relation's house.

The family, with the exception of the two younger children, were assembled in the common sitting-room.

As Frank entered, instead of the cordial welcome he had previously received, he noticed a look of coldness and constraint on the faces of Mr. and Mrs. Tarbox, while Pliny looked as if some stupendous joke was being perpetrated.

"Good-evening!" said Frank, politely. "I have been taking a walk."

"My son Pliny tells me," said Mr. Tarbox, "that you have not inherited your mother's property."

Frank bowed.

"And that it has gone to your stepfather."

"It seems so."

"I am amazed."

"So was I, sir."

"Your mother has practically disinherited you?"

"It was not my mother, sir," said Frank, hastily. "I can't explain it, but I'm sure she would not will away everything from me."

"Do you suspect your stepfather of anything irregular?" asked Mr. Tarbox, briskly.

"I would rather not answer your question, sir. I don't care to make any charges which I cannot prove."

"And so Mr. Manning has sent you out into the world to earn your own living, has he?"

"No, sir. He has consented that I may do so. It was my own plan."

Much as Frank was prejudiced against his stepfather, his natural sense of justice would not allow him to accuse him unjustly.

"Did he suggest that you should come to me?" asked Mr. Tarbox in a tone which Frank did not like.

"No, sir."

"So that was your idea, too," continued Mr. Tarbox, with a palpable sneer.

"Yes, sir," answered Frank. "You are not a very near relative, but the nearest I know of, and I supposed you would be willing to give me some advice about the best means of earning my living. I remember," he could not help adding, "that my mother received you all as guests for a considerable time, and I thought I might take the liberty."

"Oh, certainly!" returned Mr. Tarbox, rather abashed. "I am, of course, ready to give you advice, and my first advice is to seek a lawyer and let him institute a suit against your stepfather, on speculation. That is, he gets nothing if he fails, but obtains a commission if he succeeds. I could myself recommend a reliable man."

"Thank you, sir; but I have no present thought of contesting the will."

"I think you make a mistake. Do I understand that you expect to earn your own living?"

"I shall try to do so."

"You will find it very difficult. You may expect me to take you into my own store, but there is no vacancy, and——"

Frank hastily assured Mr. Tarbox that he had no such expectations. He had no wish to deprive the errand boy of the two dollars a week, which he probably richly earned.

"Situations in Newark are not easily obtained," proceeded Mr. Tarbox. "I am willing that you should stay with us a day or two, but I don't think you will find it worth your while to stay here."

Mr. Tarbox feared that his young relative might expect to find a home free of charge in his house, and such an arrangement did not suit his economical ideas. There was no profit in it, but, on the contrary, a positive loss. Frank read clearly the thoughts of his host, with the help of what Pliny had told him, and, expressing his thanks very briefly, announced his intention to go to New York the next morning.

"It may be the best thing you can do!" said Mr. Tarbox, relieved. "New York opens a much wider field to a boy of enterprise than Newark, and probably you will pick up something to do."

"It won't be my fault, if I don't," said Frank.

"You have my best wishes," said Mr. Tarbox. "The demands of my family forbid me offering you any pecuniary assistance, but ——"

"I don't stand in need of it, sir. I have money enough to keep me till I get started in something."

"Really, I am very glad to hear it!"

And there is no doubt that Mr. Tarbox was sincere.

"I wonder how much money he has got?" thought Pliny. "Perhaps he'd lend me two dollars. I'll ask him, if I have a chance."

Pliny proposed to borrow, not because he needed the money, but because he liked to levy contributions upon any available party, with a very faint idea of repaying the same. The money would go to swell his deposit at the savings-bank. It was very commendable, of course, to save his money, but not at the expense of others, as Pliny too frequently did.

"I have moved you out of the spare room," said Mrs. Tarbox, when our hero asked permission to retire, "and put you in the same room with Pliny. I suppose you won't mind?"

"Just as you please, Mrs. Tarbox," said

Frank, though he would have preferred to have passed the night alone.

"Could you make it convenient to lend me two dollars?" asked Pliny, as they went up to bed together.

"Not just now," answered Frank. "When I get something to do I shall not need to be so careful of my money."

"One dollar would answer," persisted Pliny.

Without a word, Frank drew a dollar bill from his pocket-book and handed it to Pliny.

"Now," he thought, "I shall not feel under any obligations to the family."

"You're a good fellow, even if you are poor," said Pliny, in high good humor.

Frank was tired, and it was not long before all his anxieties for the future were lost sight
all his anxieties for the future were lost sight

CHAPTER XX.

FRANK ARRIVES IN NEW YORK.

THE breakfast the next morning was very meager. It was no longer an object to gratify Frank's palate, now that he turned out to be a poor relation, and the family returned to their usual plain diet.

"So you are resolved to go to New York this morning," said Mr. Tarbox. "Of course it would gratify us to have you remain longer, but I appreciate your anxiety to get to work."

Frank was by no means deceived by this statement. He knew very well that Mr. Tarbox would be relieved by his departure, but of this knowledge he made no sign. He merely said that he thought it best to go.

He took leave of his hosts, and, purchasing a ticket at the railway station, found himself within an hour in New York. He had been there before, but it was not for a long time, and he had but a vague general idea of the city.

"Let me carry your valise," said a small boy, as he left the ferry house.

"Do you think you are any better able to carry it than I am?" asked Frank, with a smile.

"I thought you might be tired," said the street boy.

"You may take it to Broadway for me," said Frank, to whom it occurred that he might obtain some needed information from his new acquaintance. "Is this the way you make your living?" he asked.

"Sometimes I sell papers," said the boy.

"Do you get many bundles to carry?"

"Sometimes I do."

"Does it pay well?"

"Depends on the party," said the boy. "I carried a bird cage for a lady about a mile once, and she didn't want to pay me more'n five cents."

"That wasn't very liberal," Frank said.

"If I had many such customers as her, I'd soon starve to death," said the boy, in a tone of disgust.

"I've come to New York myself to earn a living," said Frank.

"Have you?" responded the boy, eying him in some surprise. "You look as if you had plenty of money."

"I have some, but I must try to earn my living. Do you know any cheap boarding-house?"

"There's a place in Mott Street where some of us boys live, but I guess it wouldn't be good enough for you."

"Where is Mott Street?"

"It ain't a very nice neighborhood. The woman lets her rooms for a dollar a week, and the boys eat at the restaurants. How much do you expect to pay for board?"

"I should like to get board for five dollars a week."

"You can get a tiptop place for that up on Bleeker Street or Clinton Place."

"How far off are these streets?"

"About two miles."

"Then come with me and show me where they are. I will pay you twenty cents an hour for your time."

"All right," said the boy, cheerfully. "Shall we walk?"

"No; we will get into the horse cars."

"Then we will take the University Place cars. There's one now."

And the boy signaled to the conductor to stop. The two boys got on board the car, and twenty minutes brought them to University Place.

As they left the car, Frank observed little slips of paper pasted on the outside of several houses with "Furnished Rooms," or "Furnished Rooms with Board," written upon them.

"I suppose I may as well inquire at some of these places," he said.

"I guess you'll get suited at some one of them," said his young guide. "Do you want me any more?"

"No, I believe not."

Frank paid the boy twenty cents and his return car fare, with which the latter seemed to be well satisfied.

He then ascended the steps of a house which purported to furnish room and board, and rang the bell.

A slipshod servant answered it.

"Have you got any small rooms?" asked Frank.

"Yes," answered the girl. "Missus is out, but I'll show you a hall bedroom, if you like."

"I should like to see it."

Frank followed the girl upstairs.

He was not favorably impressed by the appearance of the interior. He did not so much mind its being shabby, but he was repelled by the evident lack of neatness.

The girl threw open the door of a small hall

bedroom at the head of the stairs, but it looked so comfortless that he felt sure he should not like it. He thought it best, however, to inquire the price.

"Five dollars a week with board," answered the girl.

"I don't think it will suit me," said our hero.

"There's a larger room for seven dollars," said the servant.

"No. I think I will look elsewhere."

The next house was not much better, but the third was much neater and more attractive, and Frank agreed to take a room at five dollars per week.

It was a small hall bedroom, but it looked clean, and the lady who showed him about the house was very neat in her dress.

"When will you come?" asked the lady.

"Now," replied Frank, promptly.

"Would you mind paying the first week in advance?"

"Not at all. Here is the money."

And Frank drew a five-dollar bill from his portemonnaie.

"Thank you!" said the boarding-house keeper. "I have lost so much by boarders going away owing me money that I am obliged to ask gentlemen to pay in advance till I am well acquainted with them."

"That is quite right," said Frank. "What is your dinner hour?"

"Six o'clock. We have lunch at half-past

twelve for the ladies, but if any gentleman happens to be at home at that time, he can go in."

Frank looked at his watch. It was only eleven o'clock, and as so much of the day remained, he decided, as soon as he had unpacked his valise, to go downtown and look for a place without delay.

"I shall not be here at lunch to-day," he said. "You may expect me at dinner."

There was a small bureau in the room—a piece of furniture not often found in hall bedrooms.

Frank deposited the contents of the valise in the bureau drawers, and then went downstairs and out into the street.

CHAPTER XXI.

FRANK SEEKS EMPLOYMENT IN VAIN.

It was a bright, pleasant day, and Broadway looked very lively. In spite of his being alone in a strange city, with uncertain prospects, Frank felt in good spirits.

Boys of his age usually like excitement and bustle, and Frank was quick to notice the shifting scenes of the great panorama.

"Here are thousands of people," he reflected, "all of whom make a living in some way. I don't see why I can't succeed as well as they."

Some of the objects he saw amused him.

In front of him walked an elderly man with a large placard strapped to his back, on which was the advertisement of a "Great Clothing Emporium."

"I don't think I should fancy that kind of employment," thought our hero.

As he was looking in at a shop window, a boy about his own age hailed him.

"I say, Johnny, what's the price of turnips?"

"Do you want to buy any?" asked Frank, quietly.

"Well, I might. Have you got any with you?"

"I am sorry I can't supply you," said Frank, coolly. "Up our way we keep our cattle on turnips."

"You ain't so green, after all," said the boy, laughing good-naturedly.

"Thank you for the compliment!"

"I suppose I look countrylike," thought Frank, "but it won't last long. I shall get used to city ways."

Close by he saw in a window the sign:

"CASH BOYS WANTED."

Frank was not altogether certain about the duties of cash boys nor their rate of compensation, but he made up his mind not to lose sight of any chances, and accordingly stepped into the store.

It proved to be a large dry-goods store.

Near the entrance he met a tall man, with black whiskers.

"Do you want any cash boys?" inquired Frank.

"Are you inquiring for yourself?"

"Yes, sir."

"You are too large. Besides, you would not be satisfied with the wages?"

"How much do you pay, sir?"

"Two dollars a week."

"No; I don't think I should like to work for that," said Frank. "Are those cash boys?" he asked, pointing out some boys of apparently ten to twelve years old, who were flitting about from desk to counter.

"Yes."

"I see they are much younger than I. Excuse the trouble I have given you!"

"None whatever," said the man, politely.

Frank left the store, and continued his walk down Broadway.

He began to feel a little serious. It was evident that the boys did not receive as large compensation for their services as he had supposed.

It was not likely to prove an easy task to earn his own living. His board and lodging would cost him five dollars weekly; more, in fact, because he had to buy his lunch outside. Then his washing would cost him something, and there were other necessary expenses, besides clothing.

This last item might be met by the quarterly

sum with which his stepfather proposed to provide him.

The problem promised to be a perplexing one, but Frank was by no means discouraged. In fact, if he had been, he would hardly have deserved to be the hero of my story.

Though Clinton Place is not very far uptown, it is a considerable walk from this point to the Astor House.

There was so much to see, however, that Frank did not become tired, nor was he sensible of the distance. He walked a little beyond the Astor House, and, crossing Broadway, turned down Fulton Street.

On the left side of the street his attention was drawn to a restaurant, and he was led by the prompting of appetite to enter.

The prices he found to be reasonable, and the tables were already pretty well filled with clerks and business men, who were partaking of their midday lunch.

Frank found that a plate of meat, with potato and a small supply of bread and butter, could be obtained for fifteen cents.

He afterward found restaurants where the same could be gotten for ten cents, but generally there was a deficiency in quality or quantity, and there was less neatness in serving the articles.

Seated at the same table with Frank were two young men, neither probably much over twenty. One appeared to be filling a regular clerkship.

"What are you doing now, Jack?" he asked of the other.

"I am in the tea business."

"How is that?"

"You know the Great Pekin Tea Company, of course?"

"Yes."

"Well, until I can get a place, I am selling for them."

"How do you make out?"

"I can't tell you, for I have only just commenced," said his friend.

"How do they pay—salary or commission?"

"They are to pay me a commission—twenty per cent. on what I sell."

"That is a good commission."

"Yes; it is good enough, if I can make a fair amount of sales. There is a good deal of uncertainty about it, of course. I would much rather have a place like yours."

Frank listened with interest. He wondered whether the Great Pekin Tea Company would employ him. If so, he would have a field for his energy, and every inducement to work hard, since his pay would depend on the amount of his sales. Besides, as an agent, he would occupy a comparatively independent position, and Frank was ambitious enough to enjoy this.

CHAPTER XXII.

AN ADVENTURE IN WALL STREET.

When the two men at his table left the restaurant, Frank followed them. At the door the two parted, the clerk going toward Broadway, while the agent walked in the direction of Nassau Street.

"I beg your pardon," said Frank, overtaking him; "but may I ask you a question?"

"Half a dozen, if you like," said the other, good-naturedly.

"I overheard what you said about the Great Pekin Tea Company. Do you think I could get a chance to sell for them?"

"Oh, yes; there'll be no trouble about that!"

"I am looking for something to do," continued Frank, "and I think I should like to try that."

"You'll find it uphill work," said the agent; "hard work and poor pay. I shall leave it as soon as I can get a regular position. Can't you get a place?"

"Perhaps I can. I haven't tried very hard yet," answered Frank; "but I find boys are paid so little that I can't make enough to live on. If I were a man it would be different."

"I don't believe you can make more than a boy's wages at selling tea," said Frank's new acquaintance; "but you might try it."

"Would you mind giving me a note to the company?" asked Frank.

"I will write a line on one of my business cards," said the agent. "That will be all you will need."

He drew out a card and wrote a line commending Frank to the attention of the company.

Frank thanked him, and sought the direction given.

Entering a large shop, not far from the Astor House, he looked about him inquiringly. Around him were chests of tea, inscribed with Chinese characters. A portly man addressed him.

"Well, my boy, what can I do for you?" he asked.

"Mr. Mason, one of your agents, has given me this card," said Frank. "He thinks you might be willing to employ me."

"We are ready to employ any competent person," said the gentleman; "but you seem very young."

"I am sixteen, sir."

"That is young. Have you had any experience as an agent?"

"No, sir."

"What kind of business have you been in?" inquired the tea merchant.

"In none, sir."

"Do you live in New York?"

"I do now, but I only arrived this morning."

The merchant eyed Frank doubtfully.

"I suppose, then, that you don't know much about the city or the neighborhood?"

"No, sir," answered Frank, beginning to think that he had overestimated his qualifications for business.

"I am afraid, then, that you will find some difficulty."

"Let me try, sir. If I fail, or think I am likely to fail, I will give it up."

"Very well. I have no objection to your trying. Come with me."

Frank followed him to the rear of the store, where the merchant introduced him to one of his subordinates.

"Henry," said he, "this young man wants to act as our agent. Fit him out and give him such directions as may be necessary."

Frank was told that it would be well to take samples of different kinds of teas with their respective prices attached, and seek orders for them at private houses and groceries, noting down in a little book orders obtained. Small quantities he could himself deliver, and large quantities, should he be fortunate enough to obtain any, could be sent out from the store by their general delivery.

"What commission am I to get, sir?" inquired Frank.

"Twenty per cent. on parcels sold to private houses and ten per cent. when you sell to retail dealers. To the first you can charge a full price, but it is necessary to sell at lower rates to dealers."

"I understand, sir," said Frank.

"When do you want to begin?"

"To-morrow morning, sir. Where do you advise me to go?"

"New York has been pretty well canvassed, except perhaps the upper part, Harlem. It might be well to make a start in Brooklyn."

"Very well, sir. I will call to-morrow and get samples."

As Frank left the store, he reflected, with satisfaction:

"I have only been a few hours in New York, and I have gotten employment already."

This reflection raised his spirits, and disposed him to regard the future with a degree of confidence. He resolved to spend the rest of the afternoon in walking about in the lower part of the city, and acquiring a little familiarity with the streets, as this was a kind of knowledge he was likely to need.

He strolled down Broadway, admiring the massive and stately structures that lined the street on either side. Very soon he came to Trinity Church, and, standing in front of it, looked down Wall Street. He had heard so much of this street that he felt inclined to turn from Broadway and walk down its entire length.

As he sauntered along a man whom he met scrutinized him sharply, as if considering some plan. Apparently making up his mind, he stepped up to Frank, and, touching him on the shoulder, said:

"Boy, would you like a job?"

Now Frank, though he had engaged to work for the Great Pekin Tea Company, was ready to accept any other proposal, and answered promptly:

"Yes, sir."

"That is right," said the man. "It is a mere trifle, but I am willing to pay you a dollar."

"What is it, sir?"

"Do you see that window?"

He pointed to a basement window, in which were exposed rolls of gold, currency and greenbacks of different denominations, and English sovereigns and French gold coins.

"I want you to do me a little errand in there," he said.

Frank was rather surprised that the man did not do his own errand, when the broker's office was so near, but he had no objection to earning a dollar and signified his willingness.

"What I want you to do," said his new acquaintance, "is to sell some government bonds for me."

"Very well, sir."

The man produced a large yellow envelope, already open.

"In this envelope," he said, "are two five-twenty governments for a hundred dollars each. Take them in and sell them, and bring the proceeds to me."

"All right, sir."

Frank took the envelope, and entered the office of Jones & Robinson, that being the style of the firm.

He advanced to the counter, and singling out a clerk, said:

"I want to sell these bonds."

The clerk took them, and drew them out of the envelope. Then he figured a little on a slip of paper, and said:

"They are worth two hundred and twenty-five dollars and twenty-five cents."

"All right, sir."

"Will you take a check or currency?"

Frank hesitated.

"Perhaps I'd better ask the man I am getting them for."

"Very well. You can bring them here to-morrow."

"Oh, I will let you know in a minute! The man is just outside."

This answer immediately excited suspicion. Frank was too little versed in business ways to understand how singular it was for his principal not to transact his own business under the circumstances, but the brokers were necessarily keen, shrewd men.

"Wait a minute," said the clerk; "I will speak to Mr. Jones."

Mr. Jones came forward and addressed Frank.

"Are you acquainted with the man who gave you these bonds to sell?" he asked.

"No, sir. I met him in the street."

"Did he offer you any pay for selling them?"

"Yes, sir. He is going to give me a dollar."

"Will you go out and ask him to come in here a moment?"

Frank obeyed.

When his employer saw him coming, he asked, eagerly:

"Have you got the money?"

"No," answered Frank. "They asked me if I wanted a check or currency."

"Either currency or gold," answered the man, hastily. "Go back at once, and don't keep me waiting."

"They want to see you, sir."

"What for?" inquired the man, looking disturbed.

"I don't know."

"There is no need of my going in," said the man, angrily. "I paid you to sell the bonds. Now go back."

"He won't come," reported Frank. "He says I can attend to the business. He will take either gold or currency."

"No doubt," said Mr. Jones, significantly. "Thomas, go out with this boy, and tell the man that employed him that we do not purchase bonds unless we have a reasonable assurance that they belong to the person offering them. We will take the liberty of retaining them, giving him a receipt for them, and if we are satisfied, he can have his money to-morrow."

Robinson, who had been examining some newspaper slips, here came forward, and said:

"That is unnecessary. I find that these bonds are among those stolen from the house of Henry Percival, Madison Avenue, a week since. We must manage to delay the man while we notify the police."

Frank was very much surprised to learn that he was acting as agent for a bond robber, and was fearful that he might himself be regarded with suspicion; but he need not have troubled himself on this score. Wall Street men are good judges of human nature, and it was at once concluded in the office that Frank was the dupe of a designing knave.

A boy was dispatched to the nearest police office, and Frank was directed to tell his principal that he would not long be delayed.

Naturally, however, the man outside had become suspicious.

"I can't wait," he said. "Meet me on the steps of the Astor House at five o'clock with the money. I am obliged to hurry away now to a business appointment."

Frank could think of no other pretext for delaying him, and was forced to see him hurry away.

He hastened back to the office and gave the alarm.

"He has taken fright," said Robinson. "I fear we have lost him. Where did he go?"

Frank, however, was too ignorant of city streets to give any accurate information.

The consequence was that when the policeman appeared on the scene, there was no occasion for his services.

"At any rate," said the broker, "we have secured a little of the plunder. What is your name and address, my boy? We may wish to communicate with you."

Frank gave his name, and added the directions of his boarding-house.

"Shall I meet the man at the Astor House?" he inquired, as he was leaving the office.

"To be sure!" said Mr. Jones. "I came near forgetting that. Officer, will you be on hand at the time?"

"Better employ a detective, sir, as my uniform would keep the thief at a distance. I don't think he'll appear, at any rate."

"I do," said the broker. "He won't give up the money while he thinks there is a chance of securing it."

CHAPTER XXIII.

THE CAPTURE.

At the hour named, Frank repaired to the Astor House, and took a position on the steps.

He looked about him for his street acquaintance, but could see no one who bore any resemblance to him.

Finally, a man dressed in a gray suit, with a pair of green glasses, walked carelessly up to our hero and said, in a low voice:

"Have you got the money?"

Frank looked at him in surprise.

This man had thick, black whiskers, while the man who had employed him had none at all, so far as he could remember. Besides, the green glasses altered him considerably.

To make sure that he was not deceived he inquired:

"What money?"

"You know very well," said the man, impatiently. "You are the boy whom I employed to sell some bonds this morning."

"You don't look like the same man," said Frank.

"Because of my glasses. I have to wear them at times on account of the weakness of my eyes."

While he was speaking, a quiet-looking man approached and listened to the conversation.

"Then," said Frank, "you can tell me how many bonds you handed me."

"They were two five-twenty government bonds of a hundred dollars each."

"Correct, sir."

"Then hand me the money and be quick about it, for I have no time to waste! You shall have the dollar I promised you."

But here the quiet-looking man took a part in the conversation. Passing his arm through that of the man with the green glasses, he said:

"I will trouble you to come with me."

"How dare you touch me? Do you mean to insult me?" demanded the other, struggling with his captor.

"I will make all clear in due time. You must come with me and explain how you came in possession of the bonds you gave this boy."

"They were put in my hands by an acquaintance. If there is anything wrong, I am not to blame."

"In that case no harm will come to you; but now you must come along."

The other looked as if he meditated an escape, but the sight of a policeman near at hand convinced him that it would be impracticable.

"Do you want me any longer?" asked Frank.

"Not at present, but you may leave your address with me."

Frank did so; and then, feeling weary, he took a car, and, going uptown, went to his boarding-place, where he lay down for a while.

At six o'clock the dinner-bell rang, and our hero went down and took his seat at the table.

Eight persons were already in their seats—two married couples, a young lady of twenty-five, who was the teacher in one of the public schools, as Frank afterward learned, a quiet-looking, elderly man, who was a bookkeeper for a Pearl Street house, and two young men, one employed as a salesman in Stewart's retail store, and the other in a gentlemen's furnishing store on Sixth Avenue. The last mentioned was Frank's next neighbor at the table.

He was rather a dashing-looking young fellow, with his hair elaborately oiled and brushed, an incipient mustache, and a large and showy necktie.

"Ladies and gentlemen," said Mrs. Fletcher, the landlady, "this is Mr. Courtney, who has just joined our pleasant circle."

Frank made a general bow, and received a similar greeting from his fellow boarders.

"Have you just arrived in New York, Mr. Courtney?" asked the young man next him.

"Yes," answered Frank. "I only arrived this morning."

"Do you intend to remain in the city?"

"If I can find employment."

"Ah, to be sure! I hope you will. I am employed in a store on Sixth Avenue. I wish we had a vacancy. I should be glad to recommend you."

"You are very kind," said Frank.

He could not help wondering how his neighbor could feel justified in reccommending him on so brief an acquaintance, but did not think it necessary to express this.

"I suppose you have never been employed in the city, Mr. Courtney?"

"I have never been employed anywhere," admitted Frank.

"This would be against you, of course. Still, you may find an opening. By the way, Mr. Courtney, allow me to introduce myself."

The young man drew from his pocket a highly-glazed card, bearing the name, "P. Preston."

"I am glad to know you, Mr. Preston," said Frank, politely.

"You may wonder what the first letter stands for," said Mr. Preston, confidentially "Now don't be shocked when I say Peter."

"No, I am not shocked," said Frank, smiling.

"Ugly name, isn't it? I really feel that I am very badly treated in having such a name fastened upon me; but I was named for my uncle Peter."

"Where is your store?" asked Frank.

"Near Fourteenth Street. I shall be glad to see you there at any time. I suppose you are not doing anything at present."

"I have taken an agency to sell tea for the Great Pekin Company. I am to begin to-morrow."

"I am afraid you won't like it. A friend of mine tried it once and came near starving."

This was not encouraging, but Frank was not going to despair before he had fairly begun his work.

"I find that boys receive such small wages,"

Frank continued, "that I prefer to try an agency."

"Quite true," said Mr. Preston, condescendingly. "When I started I was paid a paltry sum; now I am not paid what I am worth. Still, twenty-five dollars a week is fair."

"Quite fair," responded Frank, who could not, of course, know that Mr. Preston did not receive one-half of this sum, though he chose to give that impression.

After dinner, Preston was obliged to go back to the store where he was employed. By invitation, Frank walked with him.

Turning into Sixth Avenue they passed a saloon.

"Won't you have something to drink, Courtney?" said Preston.

"No; thank you, I never drink," answered Frank.

"It will brace you up, and make you feel jolly. Better come in!"

"I don't need bracing up," answered Frank, quietly.

"Well, perhaps you are right," said Mr. Peter Preston. "I don't indulge very often, but sometimes I feel like it."

Some boys might have yielded to the temptation, but Frank had determined that he would abstain from liquor, and kept his resolution. A boy who comes to the city is exposed at every step to this peril, and needs a firm will to withstand it. It is the fruitful source of crime and misery, and does more to fill our prisons than any other cause.

"This is my store," said Preston, as he pointed to a modest-looking shop on the west side of the avenue. "I wish I could keep you company longer, but business before pleasure, you know."

Before returning to his boarding-house, Frank sat down for a short time in Washington Park, and reviewed his plans and prospects. He could not tell how he would succeed in his tea agency; but if that failed, he was resolved to try something else.

He didn't feel homesick, for since his mother's death he had no longer any home ties. Young as he was, he felt that one part of his life was at an end, and that a new life and a new career were before him.

CHAPTER XXIV.

THE YOUNG TEA MERCHANT.

THE next morning, at breakfast, one of the gentlemen, who had been running his eyes over the morning paper, said, suddenly:

"Ah! I see they have caught one of the gang who robbed the house of Mr. Percival, on Madison Avenue, a week ago."

"Read the paragraph, Mr. Smith," said one of the boarders.

Mr. Smith read as follows:

"About noon yesterday a boy entered the

banking-house of Jones & Robinson, in Wall Street, and offered for sale two one-hundred-dollar government bonds. On inquiry, he said that the bonds belonged to a man in the street, whom he had never before met, and who had offered him a dollar to sell them. This naturally excited suspicion, and a policeman was sent for. Before he could arrive the man had hastily departed, requesting the boy to meet him at a specified hour in front of the Astor House and hand him the money. He came to the rendezvous, but in disguise, and, while talking to the boy, was arrested. It is understood that he has agreed to turn State's evidence, and probably the entire sum stolen, amounting to several thousand dollars, will be recovered."

Frank listened to this paragraph with interest. He was glad that his name was not mentioned in the account, as he didn't care for such publicity. He ventured to ask a question.

"Is Mr. Percival a rich man?" he asked.

"Very rich," answered Mr. Smith. "He is not now in the city, but he is expected home from Europe in three or four weeks. His house was left in the charge of an old servant —a coachman—and his wife; but the burglars proved too much for them."

"I am glad they are caught," said Mrs. Fletcher. "It makes my blood run cold to think of having the houses entered at night by burglars."

"Preston," said Mr. Smith, jokingly, "I hope you have your bonds locked securely up."

"I don't believe the sharpest burglar can find them," said Preston. "I only wish I could get hold of them myself."

"The boy who helped to capture the burglar ought to be well rewarded," said one of the boarders.

"Don't you wish it had been you, Courtney?" said Mr. Preston.

"It was," answered Frank, quietly.

There was a great sensation upon this announcement. All eyes were turned upon our hero—most, it must be admitted, with an expression of incredulity.

"Come, now, you are joking!" said Preston. "You don't really mean it?"

"I do mean it," assured Frank.

"Tell us all about it," said Mrs. Fletcher, who had her share of curiosity. "I didn't suppose we had such a hero in our house."

"It didn't require much heroism," said Frank, smiling.

"Tell us all about it, at any rate."

Frank told the story as simply as he could, much to the satisfaction of the company.

"You'll come in for a handsome reward, when Mr. Percival gets home," suggested Mr. Smith.

"I don't expect anything," said Frank. "I

shall be satisfied if I get the dollar which was promised me. I haven't received that yet."

"I wish I were in your shoes—that's all I've got to say," said Preston, nodding vigorously. "Will you sell out for five dollars?"

"Cash down?" asked Frank, smiling.

"Well, I'll give you my note at thirty days," said the Sixth Avenue salesman, who seldom kept five dollars in advance of his liabilities.

"I won't sell what I haven't got," said Frank. "Probably I shall hear nothing from Mr. Percival."

After breakfast Frank went downtown and sought the store of the Great Pekin Company.

After half an hour's delay—for there were others in advance of him—he was fitted out with samples and started for Brooklyn.

It was his first visit to that city, but he had received some directions which made his expedition less embarrassing.

At the ferry he took a Flatbush Avenue car, and rode up Fulton Street, and passed the City Hall, up Fulton Avenue, for nearly a mile.

Here were intersecting streets, lined with comfortable houses—for Frank had made up his mind first to try private houses. He had with him a few pound parcels of tea, which he thought he could perhaps succeed in disposing of at such places.

He selected a house at random, and rang the bell.

A servant answered the ring.

Frank felt rather embarrassed, but there was no time to hesitate.

"I have some samples of tea with me," he began, "of excellent quality and at reasonable prices."

"It's no use," said the girl, abruptly. "We never buy of peddlers," and she closed the door in his face.

"Not a very good beginning," thought Frank, rather mortified. "So I am a peddler," he said to himself, and he called to mind the agents and peddlers who in past years had called at the Cedars.

With some compunction, he remembered that he had regarded them with some contempt as traveling nuisances. Now he had entered the ranks of this despised class, and he began to see that they might be perfectly respectable, and were estimable persons, animated by a praiseworthy desire to make an honest living.

Thus thinking, he called at another door.

It was opened, not by a servant, but by an elderly maiden lady, who had rather a weakness for bargains.

"I've got some nice tea," said Frank, "which I should like to sell you. It is put up by the Great Pekin Company."

"Are you sure it's nice?" asked the elderly lady. "We've been getting ours at the grocery store on the avenue, and the last wasn't very good."

"You'd better try a pound of ours," said Frank.

"I don't know but I will," said the lady. "How much do you charge?"

"I have some at fifty cents, some at sixty and some at seventy."

"I guess I'll take the sixty."

Frank had a pound parcel ready, which he delivered to her, and received his money.

"Seems to me you are pretty young for a peddler," said the lady, regarding Frank with curiosity.

"Yes, ma'am."

"How old be you?"

"Sixteen."

"Been long in the business?"

"No, ma'am; I've only just commenced."

"You don't say so! Do you make much money at it?"

"I haven't made much yet. I should be glad to supply you with some more tea when this is gone."

"Well, you can call if you are around this way. If I like it, I will try you again."

Frank's spirits rose.

His profits on the pound of tea were twelve cents. This was not much, certainly, but it was a beginning.

At the next three houses he sold nothing, being rather rudely rebuffed at one. At the fourth house, the servant called her mistress, a kind, motherly-looking woman, who seemed to regard Frank with more interest than his merchandise.

"I hope you are succeeding well," she said, kindly.

"This is my first day," said Frank, "and I have made one sale."

"I have a son who is an agent like you, but he didn't begin so young. He is now traveling in the West."

"What is he selling?" asked Frank, with interest.

"Dry goods. He travels for a wholesale house in New York."

"I suppose he is a young man."

"Yes; he is twenty-five, but he began at nineteen in a small way. He sometimes got quite discouraged at first. That is why I feel interested in any who are passing through the same experience."

These pleasant words cheered Frank. Only at the nearest house he had been called a tramp, but here he found that he was regarded with consideration.

"It is rather uphill work," said Frank.

"And you seem very young."

"I am sixteen."

"Are you entirely dependent on what you earn?" asked the lady, sympathizingly.

"Not entirely," answered the young merchant, "but I hope to make a living in this or some other way. Can I sell you any?" he asked hopefully.

"I believe we have some on hand. Still tea will always keep, and I would like to help you along."

The kind-hearted lady took three pounds—two at sixty cents and one at seventy. This gave Frank a profit of thirty-eight cents and put him in good spirits.

He worked his way back to the avenue on the other side of the street, and, coming to a grocery store, entered.

It occurred to him that he would try to sell some at wholesale.

Frank was so young that the dealer did not suppose him to be an agent, and asked what he would like to buy.

"I came to sell, not to buy," said Frank.

"What are you dealing in?" asked the grocer.

"I have several samples of tea," said our hero. "If you will give me an order, I will have it sent to you to-morrow."

The grocer found, upon examination, that his stock was getting low, and gave Frank an order, but he was obliged to sell below the regular price, and only cleared three cents a pound. Still, on a sale of twenty-five pounds, this gave him seventy-five cents, which was very encouraging.

Adding up his profits, thus far, Frank found that his commission amounted to a dollar and a quarter, which exceeded his anticipations.

He continued his calls, but sold only one

pound besides, at fifty cents, netting him ten cents more.

By this time Frank was both tired and hungry. He boarded a passing car, and, returning to Fulton Ferry, crossed to New York, relieved of the greater part of his burden. On the New York side he stepped into a restaurant, and, for twenty-five cents, secured a hearty but not luxurious lunch.

Frank repaired to the headquarters of the tea company and reported his day's sales.

"You have done unusually well," said the proprietor. "Many of our agents do not succeed in making a single sale the first day. I should not have been surprised if your experience had been similar."

"It is hard work," said Frank, "and an agent is rudely treated. Sometimes I was called a tramp and a nuisance."

The proprietor laughed.

"Hard words break no bones," he said. "The business is perfectly honorable. Will you try it again to-morrow?"

"Yes, sir, as I have nothing else to do."

"Very well; we will fit you out."

Frank took a car and went home. He found that horse cars were likely to cut largely into his profits. His expenses for the day were twenty cents for car fare and four cents for the ferry, or twenty-four cents in all. Besides this, he must count in twenty-five cents for lunch, which brought up the entire expense to forty-nine cents.

"But for the wholesale order," he reflected, "I should have cleared but eleven cents over and above expenses, while my board and washing will amount to nearly a dollar a day."

Thus Frank found that, though he had a fortunate day, he had not quite earned enough to pay his expenses.

This made him feel serious. Still, he reflected that it was only the beginning, and he might do better in the future.

CHAPTER XXV.

FRANK MEETS MR. MANNING AND MARK.

THE next morning Frank resumed his tea agency. As on the day previous, he went to Brooklyn; but, though I should be glad to say that he was more successful than on the first day, truth compels me to state that the day was a comparative failure.

It might be that he was unfortunate in the persons whom he visited, but at all events, at the close of his labors he found that his commissions amounted to less than fifty cents. He contented himself, therefore, with a ten-cent lunch, and crossed Fulton Ferry between three and four o'clock.

"This will never do," thought Frank, seriously. "I shall have to be economical to make my earnings cover my incidental expenses, while my board and lodging must be defrayed out of the money I have with me."

Frank was disappointed. It is easy to

think of earning one's living, but not quite so easy to accomplish it. A boy, besides being ignorant of the world, is inexperienced, and so disqualified for many avenues of employment which are open to men. It is generally foolish for a boy to leave a good home and start out for himself, unless the chances are unusually favorable for him. If he does it, however, he should not allow himself to be easily discouraged.

If Frank had given up the business in which he was engaged simply because he had met with one unsuccessful day, I should not have been willing to make him the hero of my story.

"This will never do," thought Frank. "I must make a greater effort to-morrow."

The next day his commission amounted to a dollar, and the fourth day to a dollar and twelve cents.

"You are doing well," said his employer. "You are doing better than the majority of our agents."

In one way this compliment was satisfactory. In another way it was not encouraging, for it limited his prospects. Frank began to think that he would never be able to make his entire expenses as a tea agent.

I do not propose to speak in detail of Frank's daily experiences, but only to make mention of any incidents that play an important part in his history.

He was returning from Jersey City on the

tenth day of his agency, when in the gentlemen's cabin he saw, directly opposite, two persons whom he had reason to remember.

They were Mark Manning and his father.

Little reason as he had to like either, they reminded him of home, and he felt pleased to meet them.

He instantly crossed the cabin, and offered his hand to his stepfather, who had not yet seen him.

"When did you arrive, Mr. Manning?" he asked.

"Why, it is Frank!" exclaimed Mr. Manning, with an appearance of cordiality. "Mark, do you see Frank?"

"Yes, I see him," replied Mark, coldly.

"Haven't you anything to say to him?" asked his father, who was much more of a gentleman than his son.

"How are you?" said Mark, indifferently.

"Thank you for your kind inquiry," said Frank, more amused than vexed, for he cared very little for his stepbrother's friendship. "I am in very good health."

"And how are you getting along?" asked his stepfather, with an appearance of interest. "Are you in any business?"

"Yes," answered Frank.

"What are you doing?" asked Mark, inspired a little by curiosity.

"I am agent for a wholesale tea house in New York," Frank answered, briefly.

"You don't say so!" exclaimed Mark, rather impressed. "What is the name of the firm?"

"The Great Pekin Tea Company."

"Does it pay well?" asked his stepbrother.

"I have met with very fair success," replied Frank.

"I congratulate you, Frank," said Mr. Manning. "Your energy and enterprise are creditable—extremely creditable. I always predicted that you would succeed—didn't I, Mark?"

"I don't remember hearing you say so," said Mark.

Mr. Manning shrugged his shoulders.

"Nevertheless," he said, "I have often made the remark."

"Where do you live?" asked Mark.

"I board in Clinton Place."

"A very respectable street," said Mr. Manning.

Frank now thought it was his turn to become questioner.

"How long do you remain in the city, Mr. Manning?" he asked.

"Not long—only a day or two," said his stepfather.

"We sail for Europe on Saturday," interposed Mark, "on the Cunard steamer."

"Indeed! I wish you a pleasant voyage."

"I am sorry you won't go with us, Frank," said his stepfather, cautiously. "You remember I gave you the chance to do so, and you desired to devote yourself immediately to business."

"Yes, sir. I would rather remain in New York."

"It might possibly be arranged now, if you desire to go," said Mr. Manning, hesitatingly.

"No, thank you, sir."

"Well, perhaps you are right," said his stepfather, considerably relieved.

"What parts of Europe do you expect to visit?" asked Frank.

"We shall visit England, France, the Rhine, Switzerland, and perhaps Italy."

"I hope you will enjoy it."

"Thank you; I think we shall."

Frank checked a sigh. It was certainly tantalizing. If he could travel with congenial friends, he felt that he would very much enjoy such a trip; but with Mark in the party there would be little pleasure for him.

"We are staying at the St. Nicholas Hotel," said Mr. Manning. "I would invite you to come and dine with us, but I have an engagement first, and don't know when we shall dine."

"Thank you, all the same," said Frank.

They had reached the New York side, and were walking toward Broadway. It was necessary for Frank to go to the tea store, and he took leave of his stepfather and Mark, again wishing them a pleasant voyage.

"I hate that boy!" said Mark, as they walked away.

"You should not indulge in any such disagreeable feelings, Mark," said his father.

"Don't you hate him?"

"Certainly not."

"One would think by your soft manner that you loved him," said Mark, who was not noted for the respect with which he treated his father.

"Really, Mark, I am shocked by your strange words."

"What made you invite him to go to Europe with us?"

"I knew he would not go."

"He might have accepted, and then we should have been in a pretty pickle."

"Mark," said his father, rather irritated, "will you be kind enough to leave me to manage my own affairs? I believe I have succeeded pretty well so far."

"Yes, you have," Mark admitted. "All the same, we'd better keep clear of Frank till we get safely off on the steamer."

CHAPTER XXVI.

A SERIOUS LOSS.

AMONG the boarders at Mrs. Fletcher's we have already named a bookkeeper. About a week after Frank's arrival, he left the house, and went further uptown. His place was supplied by a thin, dark-complexioned young man, who gave his name as Herbert Montgomery. He said, indefinitely, that he was employed in the lower part of the city, but was not communicative as to details.

This young man's room was on the same floor as Frank's, and he soon manifested a desire to become intimate with our hero.

On the third day his intimacy went so far that he asked Frank to lend him five dollars.

Now, Frank did not feel in a position to lend any one five dollars. Though he worked steadily every day, he found that his necessary expenses were making inroads upon his scanty reserve fund. Moreover, he was not attracted by Montgomery, and only responded to his advances to the extent required by politeness.

"I am sorry I cannot accommodate you, Mr. Montgomery," replied Frank.

"You don't mean to say you haven't got five dollars?" said Montgomery.

"I have got it, but I can't lend it."

"Why not?"

"It would not be convenient."

"You think you won't get it back, but you shall have it to-morrow night."

Frank could be firm when he chose to be, and he repeated his refusal.

"I don't see why you should be so disobliging," said the young man, offended.

"In the first place, it would not be convenient, and in the second, you are almost a stranger to me. Three days since I had never met you.

"Oh, if you think I am dishonest," said

Montgomery, in a tone of vexation, "I can only say that I thank you for the compliment!"

"I have not accused you of dishonesty," said Frank, calmly; "but still we are only acquaintances. What little money I have I am likely to need, for I am not yet earning enough to pay my expenses."

"Oh, well, drop the matter!" said Montgomery, checking himself suddenly. "Suppose we go out and have a game of billiards."

"Thank you, but I can't afford it."

"I'll go with you," said Preston, who overheard this proposal. "It is my evening off, and I'm in for a good time."

"Lend me five dollars, Preston—there's a good fellow," said Montgomery, transferring his attentions to the salesman.

"Do you take me for a millionaire, or do I look as if I had come in for a legacy?" said Preston, jocularly.

Nevertheless, before the evening was over he had paid out a dollar for billiards and lent his companion two dollars besides.

"Preston, you're a good fellow," said Montgomery. "You're not so mean as Courtney. I can't get a cent out of the fellow, though I promised to pay him to-morrow evening. I suppose he's got money?"

"Oh, yes; he brought a supply of money with to fall back upon, in case his business didn't pay!"

"I suppose he keeps it in the savings-bank," said Montgomery, carelessly.

"Oh, no, I guess not! He probably keeps it in his trunk. That's where I would keep my money, if I had any to keep."

It may be mentioned here that, though Frank had not brought a trunk with him to the city, he had since sent for his trunk and some extra clothing, which had been forwarded from the Cedars by his stepfather.

I do not intend to keep my readers in doubt as to the true character of Herbert Montgomery. He had no real business, and made a precarious living by running up bills at boarding houses, of which he paid as small a part as possible, and in levying tribute upon all his acquaintances by borrowing money, either with or without leave. Had Frank lent him the five dollars he asked for it would never have been returned.

He was interested in Preston's statement about Frank's reserve fund, and instantly began to consider how he could appropriate it to his own use.

The next morning he rose late, and did not breakfast till after Frank had gone downtown. Then he went leisurely to his room, and, seeing the coast clear, entered our hero's bedroom.

Closing the door and bolting it, he kneeled down by Frank's trunk, and, drawing a bunch of keys from his pocket, tried one after the other till he found one that would fit. With an exulting glance he lifted the lid and began to explore the contents.

At last he found a pocket-book, and, hastily thrusting it into his pocket, shut the trunk and relocked it. He had now accomplished what he intended, and, drawing the bolt, stepped out into the hall just as the chambermaid came up to put it in order. The girl looked at him in surprise.

"I was looking for a book which Mr. Courtney promised to lend me," he said, rather embarrassed.

"What made him lock himself up, then?" thought the girl. "I think he was there for no good."

Montgomery was a good deal annoyed by this encounter. Should Frank miss his money, it would cast suspicion upon him. He repaired to his own room, and, opening the pocket-book, discovered to his satisfaction that it contained thirty-five dollars.

"Mrs. Fletcher," he said to the landlady, five minutes later, as he descended the stairs with his valise in his hand, "I am obliged to go to Boston on business. I shall be back in a day or two. If any letters or parcels come for me, will you be obliging enough to keep them for me?"

"Certainly, Mr. Montgomery. No bad news, I hope?"

"Oh, no; only a little business trip," said Montgomery. "I am often called there."

He left the house, leaving the landlady quite unsuspicious of his reasons for going. It is hardly necessary to say that he did not go to Boston, nor did he again return to the boarding-house in Clinton Place.

Meanwhile, unlucky Frank, quite unconscious of his serious loss, was trying to sell tea in Harlem.

CHAPTER XXVII.

A DISCOURAGING DAY.

SELDOM had Frank had a more discouraging day. Of course he knew nothing of the people who lived in the houses lining the streets through which he passed. He might hit a good customer, but it was very much a matter of chance. He was more likely to find himself regarded coldly and unfavorably.

There was another obstacle of which he soon heard.

At one house, a middle-aged lady came to the door, whose face indicated a temper very easily disturbed.

"Madam," said Frank, politely, "I should like to sell you some tea."

"I dare say you would," returned the lady, in no friendly tone. "So you are a tea peddler, are you?"

Frank did not exactly like the name of peddler, for in his mind it was connected with unpleasant associations. Still, he could not refuse to be called so.

"I suppose I am," he answered.

"You suppose you are! Don't you know?" said the lady, sharply.

"I deal in tea," said Frank, rather offended.

"Who sends you out? Who do you work for?"

"The Great Pekin Tea Company."

"You do, hey! I thought so!"

"What made you think so?" Frank could not help asking.

"I'll tell you why," said the lady, aggressively. "You're the same one that came here and sold me one of your poorest kinds of tea at seventy-five cents a pound. It was an outrage and a swindle! I didn't know you at first, because I am near-sighted. And now what have you got to say for yourself, hey?"

Frank was taken aback by this unexpected accusation, and looked at the lady in surprise.

"What are you staring at, hey? You thought I wouldn't know you, but you are mistaken."

"Madam," said Frank, recovering himself, "if you have been imposed upon, I am sorry, but you must not charge me with it. This is my first visit to Harlem, and I have never seen you before in my life?"

"Do you expect me to believe that story, young man?"

"I am not in the habit of telling lies," answered Frank, with dignity.

"Do you mean to say you have never been in Harlem before?"

"Yes, I do!"

"Priscilla!" called the lady, raising her voice.

In answer, a girl about eighteen, her daughter, came downstairs.

"What's wanted, mother?"

"You remember that tea peddler that cheated me so a month ago?"

"Yes, mother."

"Take a good look at this fellow, and tell me if it is the same one."

"Certainly not, mother. This is a boy, and that was a young man with a mustache."

"Are you sure of it?"

"Certainly I am."

"I may be mistaken," said the lady, still glaring unpleasantly at Frank, "but I am not sure of it. Likely as not my daughter is mistaken and you are the same fellow after all. At any rate, you have probably played the same trick upon others."

"Oh, mother, how can you talk so?" expostulated Priscilla. "He looks like a very nice boy, I am sure."

"Thank you, miss, for your good opinion," said Frank, turning to the daughter. "I would not willingly play a trick on your mother or any one else."

"You may believe him if you want to Priscilla," said her obdurate mother, "but I've had more experience than you, and I wouldn't trust a peddler, however soft-spoken he was.

You may go away, young man, and you needn't trouble yourself to call here again."

"I certainly won't, madam," said Frank, noticing the number of the house and mentally recording it.

Frank walked away, indignant and a little discouraged.

"Certainly," he thought, "there are some disagreeable people in the world, and I have met a specimen. Her daughter looked ashamed of her, and I don't wonder at it. I don't believe all the people in Harlem are as unpleasant."

This was shown to be correct by the next lady he met.

She did not buy any tea, to be sure, but seemed sorry that she was already well supplied, and questioned Frank as to what success he was meeting with.

Frank mentioned the reception he had met with from the lady next door.

"She is a very disagreeable woman," said her neighbor. "No one likes her. Agents stand a poor chance with her. One day last week I saw her chase one out with a broom."

"Then I suppose I am lucky to have gotten off so well," said Frank, smiling.

"Yes, you were. If you should be in Harlem two or three weeks from now, I may want some tea."

"Thank you!"

When twelve o'clock came, Frank had not

sold a single pound. Even if he earned nothing, however, he had an appetite and must buy lunch.

He entered a small oyster saloon, and went up to the proprietor.

"Can I sell you some tea?" he asked.

"No, I guess not. I get my tea in Harlem."

"Take a couple of pounds," said Frank, "and I will take part of the pay in lunch."

"That is business," said the other. "Let me look at your tea."

Frank showed him his samples.

"Who employs you?"

"The Great Pekin Tea Company."

"They have a good name. Yes, I will try a couple of pounds at fifty cents."

This, of course, came to a dollar, and Frank's profit on the sale amounted to twenty cents. This was precisely the cost of the lunch which he ordered, so that he felt well satisfied with the arrangement.

He left the saloon in better spirits, and resumed his travels from house to house.

I am sorry to say, however, that though he certainly exerted himself to the utmost in the interests of the Great Pekin Tea Company and his own, he did not sell another pound of tea that day.

About three o'clock he got on board a Third Avenue horse car, bound downtown, and sat quietly down in a corner.

"Harlem doesn't seem to be a very promising field for an agent," he said to himself. "Perhaps it isn't fair to judge it by the first day. Still, I don't think I shall have courage to come here to-morrow. I would rather go to Jersey City or Brooklyn."

Frank got off the cars at the Bible House and walked to his boarding-house, where a disagreeable surprise was in store for him.

CHAPTER XXVIII.

FRANK DISCOVERS HIS LOSS.

FRANK rang the bell, finding that he had forgotten to take his pass-key with him.

The door was opened by the same girl who had detected Montgomery in Frank's room.

Frank always treated servants considerately, and Katy therefore felt well disposed toward him. She thought she ought to tell him of the morning's incident.

"Mr. Courtney," she said, as Frank was about to ascend the stairs, "did you offer to lend Mr. Montgomery a book?"

"No," answered Frank, in surprise. "What makes you ask?"

"I found him in your room this morning, with the door shut. He looked suspicious-like, but said he was after a book you promised to lend him."

"That is strange," said our hero. "I have no books with me—at any rate, none he would care to borrow. I must ask him what it means."

"You can't do that, Mr. Courtney," said Katy.

"Why not?"

"Because he's took his carpetbag and gone to Boston. He started off just after he left your room. I hope he hasn t took anything."

Katy's education had been neglected, and her language, as I hope my young readers will perceive for themselves, was not strictly grammatical.

Frank did not think of that, however. He had something else to think about.

"All my money was in my trunk," flashed through his mind.

He hastily thanked Katy for her information, and went upstairs two steps at a time. Reaching his room, he drew his key from his pocket and unlocked his trunk. He could see that the contents had been disturbed, for he was neat and orderly in his arrangements, and now the contents seemed huddled up together. He thrust his hand into the corner where he had placed his pocketbook, but his worst fears were confirmed. The pocketbook was gone!

Frank sat back in a chair, and his heart beat rapidly, as he hastily reviewed the position in which he stood.

He was not quite penniless, but nearly so. He opened his purse and examined the contents. He found that his available resources amounted to about two dollars and a half.

This would not have been so discouraging, had he been earning his expenses, but, as we know, he had not done this from the first. In four days a week's board would be due to Mrs. Fletcher, or, more properly, the advance payment for the next week.

"What shall I do?" poor Frank asked himself.

He had been trained to scrupulous honesty in money matters, and the thought that he might find himself unable to meet his obligations struck him with dismay.

"What will Mrs. Fletcher think?" he asked himself. "She may think that I am dishonest. Perhaps she may not believe that I have been robbed, but have only invented the story to impose upon her."

In this supposition, however, Frank did both himself and Mrs. Fletcher injustice, as he found when he communicated his loss to her, just before the evening meal. She exhibited great concern, and asked:

"Will this inconvenience you very much, Mr. Courtney?"

"I am afraid it will," Frank answered, soberly.

"It is a shame, I declare!" said the landlady. "I never did like that Montgomery, and I ought to have asked for references when he came here. If I had, it would have been better for you."

"Katy tells me that he has gone away"

"Yes; he told me that he was going to Boston, but a man that will steal will tell lies. I don't believe he has gone there. If he has gone anywhere, he has gone in a different direction."

In spite of his limited experience, Frank could see that this was probably the case.

"Well," he said, "it is rather hard on me, but I must see what I can do."

"I want to say, Mr. Courtney," said the warm-hearted landlady, "that I will give you plenty of time. You can stay on, and pay me when you are able. I am sure I can trust you."

"Thank you, Mrs. Fletcher!" Frank said, brightening up at these words of trust and encouragement. "I am much obliged to you, whether I need the accommodation or not. I can assure you that you will run no risk, as I have friends that I can call upon in case of necessity."

He referred to the gentleman who had purchased Ajax, and who had authorized him to draw upon him in time of need.

CHAPTER XXIX.

PERPLEXITY.

THE night brought perplexity to Frank, but not discouragement. He was naturally hopeful, and, in a large city like New York, he felt that there are always chances of obtaining employment, provided he could maintain his position, as he would have been able to do if he had not lost the thirty-five dollars which his fellow boarder had stolen. Now, however, circumstances were materially changed.

One thing was tolerably clear to Frank, and this was, that he must give up his agency. He had tried it, and been unsuccessful. That is, he had failed to earn money enough to support himself, and this was necessary.

As to what he should take up next, Frank was quite in the dark. As a boy in a counting-room he would be paid not more than four dollars a week, if he could gain such a situation, which was by no means certain.

The more he thought about the matter the more perplexed he felt, and it was in an uncomfortable frame of mind that he came down to breakfast the next morning.

By this time Frank's loss was made known to his fellow boarders.

"Have you heard anything of your friend Montgomery?" asked Preston.

"I don't think he has treated me as a friend," said Frank. "I don't believe we shall see him again very soon."

"He owes me two dollars," said Preston. "I'll sell the debt cheap."

"You won't get any bidders, Mr. Preston," said Mrs. Fletcher. "You are lucky to get off so cheap, in my opinion."

"I begin to think so myself. What are you going to do about it, Mr. Courtney?"

"I suppose I can do nothing. Montgomery has probably left the city."

Frank told no one how near he was to the bottom of his purse. He did not care to borrow money, even if he had been able to do so.

He went out as usual after breakfast and then walked leisurely downtown. He proposed to go to the shop of the Great Pekin Tea Company and resign his agency. He was on the watch during his walk for any opportunities to repair his unlucky loss:

At one place he saw a notice:

"BOY WANTED."

Though he felt sure the compensation would not be sufficient to allow of his accepting it, he thought it would do no harm to make inquiry, and accordingly entered.

It was an extensive retail store, where a large number of clerks were employed.

"Is a boy wanted here?" asked Frank of the nearest salesman.

"Yes. You may inquire at the desk."

He pointed to a desk some distance back, and Frank went up to it.

"You advertise for a boy," he said to a tall, stout man, who chanced to be the proprietor. "Is the place filled."

"No," was the answer; "but I don't think it would suit you."

"Do you think I would not be competent, sir?"

"No, that is not the difficulty. It would not be worth your acceptance."

"May I inquire what are the duties, sir?"

"We want a boy to open the door to customers, and this would not be worth your accepting."

"No, sir. Thank you for explaining it to me."

The gentleman was favorably impressed by Frank's polite and gentlemanly manners.

"I wish I had a place for you," he said. "Have you ever had any experience in our line of business?"

"No, sir; I have had very little experience of any kind. I have acted for a short time as agent for a tea company."

"You may leave your name if you like, and I will communicate with you if I have a vacancy which you can fill."

Frank thanked the polite proprietor and walked out of the store.

Though this is a story written for boys, it may be read by some business men, who will allow me to suggest that a refusal kindly and considerately expressed loses half its bitterness, and often inspires hope, instead of discouragement.

Frank proceeded to the office of the tea company and formally resigned his agency. He was told that he could resume it whenever he pleased.

Leaving the store, he walked down Broadway in the direction of Wall Street.

He passed an elderly man, with stooping shoulders and a gait which showed that he was accustomed to live in the country.

He was looking about him in rather an undecided way. His glance happened to rest on Frank, and, after a little hesitation, he addressed him.

"Boy," he said, "do you live around here?"

"I live in the city, sir."

"Then I guess you can tell me what I want to know."

"I will if I can, sir," said Frank, politely.

"Whereabouts is Wall Street?"

"Close by, sir. I am going that way, and will be happy to show you."

Frank had no idea his compliance with the stranger's request was likely to have an important effect upon his fortunes.

CHAPTER XXX.

FRANK HEARS SOMETHING TO HIS ADVANTAGE.

"My name," said the stranger, "is Peters—Jonathan Peters, of Craneville, Onondaga County. I am a farmer, and don't know much about New York. I've got a few hundred dollars that I want to put into government bonds."

"All right," said Frank, "there won't be any difficulty about it."

"I've heerd there are a good many swindlers in New York," continued Mr. Peters. "The squire—Squire Jackson, of our village—perhaps you may have heard of him?"

"I don't think I have, Mr. Peters."

"Well, the squire told me I'd better take good keer of my money, as there were plenty of rascals here who would try to cheat me out of it."

"That is true, Mr. Peters. Only yesterday I was robbed of thirty-five dollars by a man who boarded in the same house."

"You don't say so?"

"He opened my trunk and took out my pocketbook while I was absent on business."

"I wouldn't dare to live in York!" said the farmer, whose apprehensions were increased by Frank's story.

By this time they had reached the office of Jones & Robinson, with whom, it will be remembered, Frank had once before had dealings.

"If you will come in here, Mr. Peters," said our hero, "you will be sure of honorable treatment. I will introduce you if you like."

"I should be obleeged if you would," said the farmer. "Out in Craneville I am to home, but I ain't used to York business men, and don't know how to talk to them."

It pleased Frank to find that, in spite of his inexperience, he was able to be of service to one more unaccustomed than himself to city scenes and city ways.

He walked up to the counter, followed by the farmer, and said:

"This gentleman wishes to buy some government bonds. I told him that he could transact his business here."

"Thank you! Mr. Benton, you may attend to this gentleman."

Frank was about to leave the office, when Mr. Robinson called him back.

"You have been in the office before, have you not?" he asked.

"Yes, sir."

"Are you not the boy who assisted in the capture of the man who robbed Mr. Henry Percival, of Madison Avenue?"

"Yes, sir."

"I thought so. I have been trying to find you for the last week."

Naturally Frank looked surprised.

"Mr. Henry Percival was at that time in Europe," said Mr. Robinson. "On his return, a week since, he called on us, and expressed a desire to have you call upon him. We had mislaid or lost your address, and were unable to give him the information he desired."

Frank's heart beat high with hope as the broker spoke.

"Perhaps," he thought, "Mr. Percival may offer me a situation of some kind, and I certainly am greatly in need of one."

"Did Mr. Percival recover all his bonds?" he asked.

"Nearly all," answered Mr. Robinson. "He considered himself exceedingly fortunate, and he certainly was so.

"Do you know how much he was robbed of?" asked Frank.

"Rather over five thousand dollars. Of this sum all has been recovered except three bonds of a hundred dollars each. Mr. Percival is a rich man, and he won't miss that small amount."

"I wish I were rich enough not to miss three hundred dollars," thought our hero. "If I had my rights, I could say the same."

Just now, in his extremity, Frank thought regretfully of the fortune he had lost. Had he been so situated as to be earning enough to defray all his expenses, he would scarcely have given a thought of it.

"You had better go up to see Mr. Percival this evening," said the banker, "if you have no other engagement."

"Even if I had an engagement, I would put it off," said Frank. "Will you give me Mr. Percival's number?"

"No. 265," said Mr. Robinson.

Frank noted it down and left the office. By this time Mr. Peters had completed his business, and was ready to go out, also.

"I'm much obliged to you," he said to Frank. "I was afraid I'd get into a place where they'd cheat me. I guess Mr. Jones and Robinson are pretty good folks."

"I think you can depend upon them," said Frank.

"If ever you come to Craneville, I should

like to have you stay a few days with me on my farm," said Mr. Peters, hospitably. "We are plain folks, but will treat you about right."

"Thank you, Mr. Peters. If I ever come to Craneville, I shall certainly call upon you."

Though Frank was so near the end of his money, he had something to look forward to in his approaching interview with Mr. Percival. He had been able to do this gentleman a service, and it was not unlikely that the capitalist would wish to make him some acknowledgment. Frank did not exaggerate his own merits in the matter. He felt that it was largely owing to a lucky chance that he had been the means of capturing the bond robber. However, it is to precisely such lucky chances that men are often indebted for the advancement of their fortunes.

While he was in a state of suspense, and uncertain what Mr. Percival might be disposed to do for him, he decided not to exert himself to obtain any employment. If he should be disappointed in his hopes, it would be time enough to look about him the following day.

What should he do in the meantime?

He determined to treat himself to an excursion. From the end of the Battery he had often looked across to Staten Island, lying six miles away, and thought it would prove a pleasant excursion. Now, having plenty of time on his hands, he decided to go on board one of the boats that start hourly from the piers adjoining the Battery. The expense was but trifling and, low as Frank's purse was, he ventured to spend the amount for pleasure. He felt that he needed a little recreation after the weeks of patient labor he had spent in the service of the Great Pekin Tea Company.

CHAPTER XXXI.

MR. MONTGOMERY TURNS UP AGAIN.

It was a pleasant day, and as Frank steamed out of the harbor, passed the fort, but a mile distant, and from the deck of the ferryboat observed the vessels of every description darting here and there on their various courses, he felt quite cheerful.

"If I can only maintain myself here," he thought to himself, "I shall be contented and happy. I would a great deal rather be usefully employed than travel in Europe with Mr. Manning and Mark."

The first landing, about six miles distant, was at New Brighton. The island looked very attractive, with its hilly shores dotted with handsome villas, standing in the midst of trees.

The boat made a brief stop and proceeded successively to Castleton, Port Richmond and Elm Park. This Frank found to be the last stopping place, and he landed, in company with many others.

A steep path led him to a hotel and adjoining park, in which were set tables for the accommodation of lunching parties. There were swings between tall trees and other arrangements for the pleasure of visitors. From the upper part of the inclosure there was a fine view of the water and places in the vicinity.

Frank sauntered about, enjoying himself in a quiet way. He assisted to swing some young children, with whom he became pleasantly acquainted.

When the next boat came in, Frank idly watched the faces of the passengers as they entered the park, not thinking it very likely, however, that he should see any familiar face. He was destined to be surprised.

Strolling along, in a very complacent mood, came a young man whom he had good cause to remember.

It was Herbert Montgomery, who had robbed him of his little stock of money.

Frank's face lighted up with surprise and pleasure. He strongly doubted whether he should recover any of his money, but he would, at any rate, have the satisfaction of expressing to Mr. Montgomery his opinion of his conduct.

"Mr. Montgomery," he said, quietly, "I should like a little conversation with you."

Montgomery turned suddenly. When he saw Frank, he looked startled and even dismayed. But he quickly recovered his self-possession, and decided upon his course.

"I beg your pardon, my boy," he said. "Were you addressing me?"

Frank was a boy, but to be addressed in this

patronizing way by the man who had injured him did not suit his ideas.

"I did address you, Mr. Montgomery," he said. "I will thank you to return me the thirty-five dollars you took from my trunk without leave. By so doing, you will save yourself trouble."

"Boy," said Montgomery, loftily, "I don't know whether you are drunk or crazy, but I am quite sure you must be one or the other. What can induce you to address an utter stranger in such insulting terms I cannot guess. I decline to have anything further to say to you."

"An utter stranger!" repeated Frank, in the greatest amazement.

"I repeat that you are an utter stranger to me," said Montgomery, with unblushing effrontery. "I never, to my knowledge, set eyes on you before this morning."

"Do you mean to deny that your name is Herbert Montgomery?" asked Frank.

"I certainly do. I never heard the gentleman's name before."

"Do you mean to deny that you have been boarding at the house of Mrs. Fletcher, in Clinton Place?"

"I certainly do."

"Perhaps," said Frank, not believing his statement, "you will tell me what your name is?"

"Certainly. My name is Ephraim Parker, at your service."

"How long has it been so?" inquired Frank.

"Young fellow," said Montgomery, "I don't know who you are, but you are certainly very impertinent. If you have really lost any money, I am sorry for you, but it is nothing to me. This Herbert Montgomery, or whatever his name may be, may possibly look like me. I am not responsible for any accidental resemblance. Good-morning! and be careful next time before you insult a gentleman on an uncertainty."

It had never fallen within Frank's experience to meet a man so utterly reckless of truth, and he asked himself whether he might not be mistaken. He had heard of cases of resemblance so great that people were mistaken even by near friends for each other. Was it possible that the man before him was a case in point?

He scanned Montgomery's face carefully, and detected a lurking smile of exultation, accompanied by a characteristic lifting of the eyebrow. This satisfied him. It was Montgomery, and not Parker.

"Mr. Montgomery," he said, "I know you very well. You cannot impose upon me. I ask you again to return me my money, or as much as you have left."

"Leave me!" said Montgomery, angrily. "I have had enough of your impertinence. I am a gentleman from Chicago, temporarily in New York on business. I have wasted time enough on you already."

"Good-by for the present, Mr. Montgomery," said Frank. "I think the time will come when I shall be able to unmask you."

Montgomery walked off in seeming indifference, but he was very glad to see Frank leave by the next boat.

"I don't want to meet that boy again," he muttered. "It was a close shave, and required all my impudence to get rid of him. Probably I had better leave New York for a time."

He followed Frank back to the city by the next boat, and that afternoon embarked on the Fall River boat for Boston.

CHAPTER XXXII.

AN INCIDENT IN A STREET CAR.

When Frank returned to New York after his unsatisfactory interview with Montgomery, he felt annoyed and provoked. To have lost his money was bad enough, but to be treated with such cool impudence by the thief was quite as disagreeable. Had Montgomery admitted his guilt and showed penitence, or pleaded poverty, Frank would have been willing to overlook his offense, for he was of a generous nature; but to be openly denied made him angry.

Besides, he could not help reflecting seriously on the strait he was in. He was almost penniless, and knew not where to look for a fresh supply of money. At the end of the quarter he was authorized by his stepfather to call for twenty-five dollars, but this was still some weeks distant, and in the meantime he must either earn enough to defray his expenses or run into debt. There was, however, one hope—that Mr. Percival might give him employment—and this would probably be decided that same evening.

When Frank reached the city, he walked slowly up through the Battery to the foot of Broadway. He passed the famous house, No. 1, which, a hundred years ago, was successively the headquarters of Washington and the British generals, who occupied New York with their forces, and soon reached the Astor House, then the most notable structure in the lower part of the city.

With his small means, Frank felt that it was extravagant to ride uptown, when he might have walked, but he felt some confidence in the success of his visit to Mr. Percival, and entered a Fourth Avenue horse car. It so chanced that he seated himself beside a pleasant-looking young married lady, who had with her a young boy about seven years old.

Soon after the car started the conductor came around to collect the fares.

Frank paid his, and the conductor held out his hand to the lady.

She put her hand into her pocket to draw out her purse, but her countenance changed as her hand failed to find it.

Probably no situation is more trying than to discover that you have lost or mislaid your purse, when you have an urgent use for it. The lady was evidently in that predicament. Once more she searched for her purse, but her search was unavailing.

"I am afraid I have lost my purse," she said, apologetically, to the conductor.

This official was an ill-mannered person, and answered, rudely:

"In that case, ma'am, you will have to get off."

"I will give you my card," said the lady, "and will send double the fare to the office."

"That won't do," said the man, rudely. "I am responsible for your fare, if you stay on the car, and I can't afford to lose the money."

"You shall not lose it, sir; but I cannot walk home."

"I think you will have to, madam."

Here Frank interposed. He had been trained to be polite and considerate to ladies, and he could not endure to see a lady treated with rudeness.

"Take the lady's fare out of this," he said.

"And the boy's, too?"

"Of course."

The lady smiled gratefully.

"I accept your kindness, my young friend," she said. "You have saved me much annoyance."

"I am very glad to have the opportunity," said Frank, politely.

"Of course, I shall insist upon reimbursing

you. Will you oblige me with your address, that I may send you the amount when I return home?"

A boy of less tact than Frank would have expostulated against repayment, but he knew that this would only embarrass the lady, and that he had no right, being a stranger, to force such a favor upon her. He answered, therefore:

"Certainly, I will do so, but it will be perfectly convenient for me to call upon you."

"If it will give you no trouble, I shall be glad to have you call any evening. I live at No.—— Madison Avenue."

Now it was Frank's turn to be surprised. The number mentioned by the lady was that of the house in which Mr. Henry Percival lived.

"I thought Mr. Percival lived at that number?" said Frank.

"So he does. He is my father. Do you know him?"

"No; but I was about to call on him. This morning Mr. Robinson, a broker in Wall Street, told me that he wished to see me."

"You are not the boy who caused the capture of the bondholder?" asked the lady, quickly.

"Yes, I am the boy, but I am afraid I had less to do with it than has been represented."

"What is your name?"

"Frank Courtney."

"My father is very desirous of meeting you,

and thanking you for what you have done. Why have you not called before?"

"I did not know till to-day that your father had returned. Besides, I did not like to go without an invitation."

"I will invite you," said the lady, with a pleasant smile, "and I, as well as my father, will be glad to see you. And now let me introduce you to my little son. Freddie, would you like to see the boy that caught the robber?"

"Yes, mamma."

"Here he is. His name is Frank."

The little boy immediately began to ask questions of Frank, and by the time they reached the Cooper Institute Frank and he were well acquainted.

"Don't get out, Frank," said Freddie.

"I am going home, Freddie."

"You must come and see me soon," said the little boy.

"Now you have three invitations," said the lady.

"I will accept them all," said Frank.

And, with a bow, he left the car.

CHAPTER XXXIII.

FRANK MAKES AN EVENING CALL.

AFTER supper Frank walked slowly up to Mr. Percival's residence. Now that he knew two members of the family, he looked forward with pleasure to the call he was about to make. His prospects seemed much brighter than when he woke up in the morning, and the annoyance of his meeting with Montgomery was nearly effaced by his pleasant encounter in the horse car.

On reaching the house of Mr. Percival, he saw at a glance that it was the residence of a wealthy man, and the hall, into which he was first admitted, was luxurious in its appearance. But Frank had been brought up to the enjoyment of wealth, and he felt more at home here than in the rather shabby boarding-house in Clinton Place.

A colored servant opened the door.

"Is Mr. Percival at home?" he asked.

"Yas, sah."

"I should like to see him."

"What name, sah?"

"Frank Courtney."

"Step in, sah, and I will 'form Mr. Percival," said the colored servant, in a consequential tone that amused Frank.

Frank stepped into the hall, but he was not left long without attention. Little Freddie ran downstairs, eagerly calling out:

"Did you come to see me, Frank?"

"Yes," answered Frank, smiling; "but I came to see your grandfather, too."

"Come, and I will show you where he is," said the little boy, taking Frank's hand.

The two went up the staircase and into a handsomely furnished room, made attractive by pictures and books.

In a large armchair sat a pleasant-looking elderly man, of about sixty.

"Grandpa," said the little boy, "this is Frank. He wants to see you."

Mr. Percival smiled.

"I am glad to see you, Frank," he said. "It seems, my boy, that you are already acquainted with my daughter and grandson."

"Yes, sir. I was fortunate enough to meet them to-day."

"You relieved my daughter from some embarrassment."

"I am glad to have had the opportunity, sir."

Frank's manner was easy and self-possessed, and it was evident that Mr. Percival was favorably impressed by him.

"Take a seat," he said, "while I ask you a few questions."

Frank bowed and obeyed."

"Let me sit in your lap, Frank," said Freddie.

Our hero took the little boy in his lap.

With Freddie, it was certainly a case of friendship at first sight.

"Won't he trouble you?" asked his grandfather.

"No, sir. I like young children."

Mr. Percival now proceeded to interrogate Frank.

"Your name is Frank Courtney. Have you been long in the city?"

"No, sir; only a few weeks."

"What led you to come here?"

"I wish to earn my own living."

"Was that necessary? You do not look like a poor boy."

"I was brought up to consider myself rich," said Frank.

"Indeed! Did you lose your property?"

"Perhaps I had better tell you how it happened, sir."

"If you don't object, I should be glad to hear."

Frank gave a brief statement of his position, and the circumstances that led him to leave his home and go out into the world.

Mr. Percival listened thoughtfully.

"It is a singular story," he said, after a pause. "Your stepfather's in Europe, then?"

"Yes, sir; at least he sailed for Europe."

"Have you heard from him?"

"No, sir."

"Do you expect to hear?"

"I think not."

"He can't feel much interest in you."

"I don't think he does," answered Frank. "Still, I can't say that he has treated me unkindly."

"Do you suspect that your stepfather has wronged you in the matter of the property?"

"I would rather not answer that question, sir. I might wrong Mr. Manning, and I have no proof to offer."

"I understand you, and I applaud your discretion. It does you credit. Some time or other the mystery may be cleared up, and the wrong, if there is one, may be righted. I can't understand, however, how this Mr. Manning should be willing to leave you dependent upon your own exertions with such a scanty provision as twenty-five dollars a quarter."

"I didn't ask for any more; and, besides, Mr. Manning offered to take me to Europe with his son Mark."

"Do you think that he was sincere in the offer?"

"I don't think he expected me to accept it, and I am sure that it would have been very disagreeable to Mark to have me in the party."

"Have you any objections to telling me how you have succeeded in your efforts to make a living?" asked the old gentleman, with a keen but kindly glance.

"I have been disappointed, sir," was the candid reply.

"I am not surprised to hear it. A boy brought up as you have been cannot rough it like a farmer's son or a street boy."

"I think I could, sir; but I should not like to."

"Precisely. Now, I am not sure that you acted wisely in undertaking a task so difficult, since it was not necessary, and your stepfather could hardly have refused to support you at home. However, as you have taken the decisive step, we must consider what is best to do under the circumstances. What work have you been doing?"

"I have been selling tea for the Great Pekin Tea Company."

"How have you succeeded?"

"I have not been able to pay expenses," Frank admitted.

"How have you made up the difference?"

"I brought about fifty dollars with me from home."

"Is it all used up?"

"I had thirty-five dollars left, sir, but a day or two since one of my fellow boarders opened my trunk and borrowed it without leave."

"Of course you won't recover it?"

"I don't think there is much chance of it, sir."

"Then probably your money is nearly exhausted?"

Frank did not like to admit his poverty, but owned up that he had less than two dollars.

"And yet you paid the car fares of this little boy and his mother?"

"I hope, sir, I would not refuse to assist a lady when in trouble."

Mr. Percival nodded two or three times, smiling as he did so. He was becoming more and more favorably impressed with our young hero.

"Do you mean to continue this tea agency?" he asked.

"No, sir; I have already notified my employers that I do not care to continue it."

"Have you anything else in view?"

Frank felt that now was the time to speak.

"I came here this evening," he said, "intending to ask you if you knew of any situation I could fill, or could recommend me to employment of any kind by which I might make a living."

"I must consider that. Have you thought of any particular employment which you would like?"

"No, sir; I cannot afford to be particular. I will do anything that is honest, and at all suitable for me."

"What would you consider unsuitable?"

"I should not wish to black boots, for instance, sir. It is honest work, but I ought to be suited to something better."

"Of course! What education have you had? Good, I suppose?"

"I am nearly ready for college."

"Then you are already fairly well educated. I will put you to a test. Sit up to the table, and take paper and pen. I will dictate to you a paragraph from the evening paper, which I should like to have you write down."

Frank obeyed, though, in doing so, he was obliged to set Freddie down, rather to the little fellow's dissatisfaction.

Mr. Percival selected a short letter, written by some public man, which chanced to have found a place in the evening journal.

Frank wrote rapidly, and when his copy was finished, submitted it to Mr. Percival.

The old gentleman took it, and, running his eye over it, noticed that it was plainly written, correctly spelled and properly punctuated. This discovery evidently gave him satisfaction.

"Very creditably written," he said. "I have known boys nearly ready for college who could not copy such a letter without blundering. I am glad that your English education has not been neglected while you have been studying the classics."

Frank was gratified by Mr. Percival's commendation, though he could not see in what manner his education was likely to bring him employment. It was desirable, however, to produce a favorable impression on Mr. Percival, and he could not help hoping something would result to his advantage.

At this moment Freddie's mother entered the room, and greeted Frank with a cordial smile.

"Freddie," she said, "it is time for you to go to bed."

"I don't want to leave Frank," said Freddie.

"Frank will come and see you again."

"Will you, Frank?"

Frank made the promise, and Mrs. Gordon—for that was her name—left the room, promising to return before Frank went away.

He was now left alone with the old gentleman.

CHAPTER XXXIV.

FRANK IS OFFERED A POSITION.

MR. PERCIVAL engaged Frank in conversation on general topics while Mrs. Gordon was out of the room. His young visitor had been an extensive reader, and displayed a good deal of general information. Moreover, he expressed himself intelligently and modestly, and deepened the favorable impression which he had already succeeded in making.

I should like to call the attention of my young readers to the fact that Frank was now reaping the advantage of the time he had devoted to study and the cultivation of his mind.

A boy who starts in life with a fair education always stands a better chance than one who is poorly provided in that respect.

It is true that many of our prominent public men have started with a very scanty supply of book-learning, but in most cases it has only transferred the labor of study to their maturer years.

President Andrew Johnson did not learn to read and write until after he had attained his majority, but he made up his early deficiencies later.

Abraham Lincoln, when nearly thirty, devoted his leisure hours to mastering the problems in Euclid. and thus trained and strengthened his mental faculties so that he was enabled to grapple with the difficult problems of statesmanship in after years.

Henry Wilson commenced attending an academy after he had reached the age of twenty-one.

The fact is, no boy or man can be too well equipped for his life-work.

I hope my boy readers will not skip the paragraphs above, for they can learn from them a useful lesson.

When Mrs. Gordon returned, she placed in Frank's hands a small sum of money, saying:

"Allow me to repay my debt, with many thanks."

"You are quite welcome," answered our hero.

He had too much tact to refuse the money, but quietly put it into his pocket.

"Helen," said Mr. Percival, "I would like a word with you. We will leave our young friend here alone for five minutes."

"Certainly, father."

The two went into an adjoining room, and Mr. Percival commenced by asking:

"How do you like this boy, Helen?"

"Very much. He seems to have been brought up as a gentleman."

"He has. Till a short time since he supposed himself the heir to a fortune."

"Indeed!" said Mrs. Gordon, with curiosity.

Briefly, Mr. Percival rehearsed the story which Frank had told him.

"What a shame!" exclaimed Mrs. Gordon, indignantly. "His stepfather ought to be punished."

"That may come in time. Wickedness does not always prosper. But as regards our young friend, I have a plan in view."

"What is it, father?"

"I find he has an excellent education, having been nearly ready for college when the crisis in his fortunes came. I have been thinking whether we could not find a place for him in this house. My eyes, you know, are so weak that they are often strained by attention to my correspondence and reading. I have an idea of engaging Frank Courtney as a sort of private secretary, upon whom I can at any time call. Of course, he would have his home in the house."

"There will be no difficulty about that. Our family is small, and we have plenty of vacant rooms. But, father, will he be qualified to undertake the duties you have designed for him? He is very young."

"That is true, my dear; but he is remarkably well educated. I have tested his capacity by dictating a letter for him to copy."

"Did he do the work satisfactorily?" asked Mrs. Gordon.

"Without a single mistake."

"Then, father, I would not hesitate to engage him. Freddie likes him, and will be delighted to have him in the house."

"Another idea, Helen. It is time Freddie began to study. Suppose we make him Freddie's private tutor—say for an hour daily?"

"That is really an excellent idea, father," said Mrs. Gordon, in a tone of satisfaction. "It will please and benefit Freddie, and be a relief to me. Do you think Frank will have patience enough?"

"I watched him with the little fellow, and I could see that he liked children. I am sure he will succeed in this as well as in the duties which he will undertake for me."

"I suppose he will have no objection to the plan?"

"I think he will accept gladly. He has had a hard struggle thus far in maintaining himself, and I can relieve him from all anxiety on that score. I am indebted to him for helping me to recover my bonds, and this will be an excuse for offering him a larger salary than the services of so young a secretary could be expected to command."

"Very well, father. Your plan pleases me very much, and I shall be glad to have Frank commence to-morrow, if he chooses. Now let us return to the library."

While father and daughter were absent Frank had taken from the table a volume of "Macaulay's History," and had become interested in it.

He laid it down upon their return.

Mr. Percival resumed his easy-chair, and said, with a smile:

"My daughter and I have been consulting about you."

Frank bowed, and his hopes rose.

"I suppose you are open to an offer of employment?"

"I am not only open to it, Mr. Percival, but I shall be grateful for it."

He could not help wondering what sort of employment Mr. Percival was about to offer him. He concluded that it might be a place in some business house.

"The fact is," said the old gentleman, "I have a great mind to offer you the situation of my private secretary."

Frank was astonished. This was something he had not thought of.

"Do you think I am qualified to fill such a position, Mr. Percival?" he asked, hesitatingly.

"The duties would not be difficult," returned the old gentleman. "Though not in active business, the care of my property, and looking after my scattered investments, involves me in considerable correspondence. My eyes are not as strong as they once were, and I find them at times taxed by letter-writing, not to mention reading. You can relieve me very materially."

"I shall be very glad to do so, sir. The duties will be very agreeable to me."

"But that is not all. My daughter proposes to employ you as private tutor for Freddie."

Frank smiled.

"I think my scholarship will be sufficient for that," he said.

"Freddie likes you," said Mrs. Gordon, "and if you think you would have patience enough——"

"I think I should," assured Frank. "I was always fond of children, and Freddie is a very attractive boy."

"I believe he has an equally favorable opinion of you," said Mrs. Gordon, smiling.

"We are very good friends, I think," said Frank.

"Then I am to understand that you will not object to this double position?" said Mr. Percival.

"I shall be very glad to accept," said Frank, promptly.

"Of course, you will need to make your home with us," said the old gentleman. "My daughter will assign you a room, and you may move in as soon as you like."

"That will be to-morrow, sir."

"I like your promptness. There remains one thing to be considered. We have not settled about the amount of your salary."

Salary sounded well, and Frank began already to feel himself a young man.

"I will leave that entirely to you, sir," he said.

"Will fifty dollars a month satisfy you?" asked Mr. Percival, with a benevolent smile.

"Fifty dollars a month, besides my board?" ejaculated Frank.

"Yes."

"But I am sure I cannot earn so much," said Frank, candidly.

"It is, I am aware, more than would usually be offered to a boy of your age; but I owe you something for the service you rendered me, in helping me to recover my bonds. I have not offered you any pecuniary recompense, thinking you would prefer employment."

"You judged rightly, sir, and I feel very grateful to you."

"I did not think, this morning," said Mrs. Gordon, smiling, "that I should find a tutor for Freddie before night."

"It is rather a surprise to me," said Frank, "but a very agreeable one. I feel very much indebted to you both for the confidence you feel in me, and I will now bid you good-evening!"

"One minute, Frank," said Mr. Percival. "Would it be convenient for you to receive a month's salary in advance?"

"I shall not need the whole of it, sir; but if you will let me have twenty dollars, I can easily wait for the balance till the end of the month."

Mr. Percival drew from his pocketbook twenty dollars in bills and placed them in the hands of his young visitor.

Frank thanked him earnestly.

"We shall expect to see you to-morrow," said Mr. Percival. "Good-night."

Frank left the house in high spirits. He had found strong friends, and secured a position and a salary beyond his highest expectations. He determined to do his best to satisfy his employer.

CHAPTER XXXV.

FRANK AS PRIVATE SECRETARY.

THE next day Frank transferred his residence to Madison Avenue. He was assigned a pleasant room, decidedly superior, it need hardly be said, to his room at Clinton Place. It seemed agreeable to him once more to enjoy the comforts of a liberal home.

Frank had had some doubts as to how he would satisfy Mr. Percival in his capacity of private secretary.

He was determined to do his best, but thought it possible that the old gentleman might require more than he could do well. He looked forward, therefore, with some apprehension to his first morning's work.

Mr. Percival, though not engaged in active business, was a wealthy man, and his capital was invested in a great variety of enterprises. Naturally, therefore, he received a large number of business letters, which required to be answered.

The first day he dictated several replies, which Frank put upon paper. He wished, however, to put Frank's ability to a severe test.

"Here are two letters," he said, "which you may answer. I have noted on each instructions which you will follow. The wording of the letters I leave to you."

"I will try to satisfy you, sir," said Frank.

Our hero was a good writer for his age. Moreover, he had been well trained at school and did not shrink from the task assigned him.

He read carefully the instructions of his employer, and composed the letter in strict accordance with them.

Mr. Percival awaited with some interest the result of his experiment. If Frank proved competent to the task assigned him, his own daily labor would be considerably abridged.

"Here are the letters, sir," said our hero, passing the drafts to Mr. Percival.

The old gentleman examined them carefully. As he did so, his face expressed his satisfaction.

"Upon my word, Frank," he said, familiarly, "you have done your work exceedingly well. They are brief, concise and yet comprehensive. I feared that you would use too many words."

"I am glad you are pleased, sir. Dr. Brush trained us to write letters, and he cut down our essays when they were too diffuse."

"Then I feel indebted to Dr. Brush for providing me with so competent a young secretary. You will be able to assist me even more than I anticipated. I shall, of course, read over your letters before they are sent, to make sure that you have fully comprehended and carried out my instructions, but I don't expect they will need much correction."

Frank was much gratified by these words. This was the only point on which he had felt at all doubtful as to his ability to please his employer.

Sometimes, when his eyes pained him more than usual, Mr. Percival also employed him to read to him from the daily papers, or from some book in which he was interested, but this did not occur regularly.

Every day, however, Frank was occupied with Freddie. The little boy knew his alphabet, but nothing more, so that his young teacher had to begin with him at the beginning of the primer.

He succeeded in interesting his little pupil, and did not protract his term of study so as to weary him.

Finding that the little fellow was fond of hearing stories, he read to him every day a story or two from Hans Christian Andersen, or from a collection of German fairy stories, and sometimes went out to walk with him.

Freddie was delighted with his teacher, and freely expressed his approval to his mother and grandfather.

"Really, Frank," said Mrs. Gordon, "I shall begin to be jealous of your hold upon Freddie. I am not sure but he likes your company better than mine."

"I don't think Freddie will prefer anyone

to his mother," said Frank; "but I am glad he likes to be with me."

"You have certainly proved very successful as a private tutor, Frank," said Mrs. Gordon, "and my father tells me you succeed equally well as a secretary."

"It is partly because you both treat me so indulgently," answered Frank, gracefully.

This answer pleased Mr. Percival and Mrs. Gordon, who more than ever congratulated themselves upon the lucky chance that had thrown Frank in their way.

Assuredly he made himself very useful in the small household, contributing to the comfort and pleasure of Freddie, his mother and grandfather in nearly equal measure.

While Frank's monthly salary was of great value and importance to him, it was nothing to Mr. Percival in comparison with the pleasure and relief afforded by his presence in the house.

It must not be supposed, however, that Frank's time was wholly occupied by the duties of his two positions. Usually he had several hours daily at his disposal, and these he was allowed to spend as he pleased.

Part of this he occupied in visiting different localities of the city and points of interest in the neighborhood, and part in reading and study.

Mr. Percival had a large and well-selected library, which, to a boy of Frank's studious taste, was a great attraction.

He entered upon a course of solid reading, embracing some of the standard histories, and devoted some hours every week to keeping up his acquaintance with the Greek and Latin authors which he had read at school.

In this way his time was well and usefully employed, and the weeks slipped by till almost before he was aware six months had passed. The next chapter will record a meeting with some old acquaintances.

CHAPTER XXXVI.

PLINY TARBOX.

ONE afternoon Frank walked down Broadway, enjoying the bright sunshine and the animated spectacle which the leading New York thoroughfare always presents. He had completed his duties for the day, and felt at leisure to enjoy himself. He was no longer in any pecuniary embarrassment, having saved up one hundred and fifty dollars out of the salary paid him by Mr. Percival.

Besides this, he had two quarterly payments from his stepfather's banker. He had decided not to call for this money, but on consulting his employer, he had changed his mind.

Mr. Percival represented that he need feel no scruples about taking what was, after all, but a small part of what he was entitled to, even admitting the will to be genuine, since Mr. Manning was expressly directed to provide for him.

Frank was wise enough to be guided by a man whose experience was so much greater than his own, and drew the money. He had, therefore, at present, two hundred dollars in all, which he had deposited in a savings-bank recommended to him by Mr. Percival.

Now, two hundred dollars was but a very small sum compared with the fortune he had lost, but its possession gave Frank much satisfaction. Three-fourths of it he had himself earned and this was a source of pleasure and comfort.

If boys and young men who squander their money would change their habits for a single month, and lay aside what hitherto they had lavished on unnecessary expenses, they would experience a satisfaction which would go far toward inducing them to continue their economy.

Frank had been obliged to make some purchases of clothing, since, as an inmate of such a house, he felt that he would be expected to dress well. Yet, over and above all expenses, he had saved, as I have said, two hundred dollars. Had such a sum been given him, he might have felt more disposed to spend it foolishly; but a boy who earns money knows better how to value it.

Then, as Frank walked down Broadway, he was able to resist the temptations that allured him from many a shop window without an effort.

Just in front of the St. Nicholas Hotel he heard his name called.

Looking up, he recognized, with some surprise, Pliny Tarbox, his cousin from Newark, whom he had not seen since his hurried departure from a house where his changed fortunes had made him unwelcome.

"Is it you, Pliny?" he asked.

"Yes."

"Are you in business here?"

"No. I am still in the bookstore. I came to New York to buy some clothes. I thought I could get them cheaper here than in Newark. Father makes me buy my own clothes out of my wages. Don't you think that mean?"

"I should not like to make such a charge against your father, Pliny."

"Oh, he is mean—awful mean! Everybody knows that," said Pliny, apparently not aware that it did him little credit to speak so of his father.

"Is it such a hardship to pay for your own clothes?" said Frank. "I not only pay for my own clothes, but I pay all my expenses, with the help of only two dollars a week from my stepfather."

This drew Pliny's attention to his cousin.

"You're pretty nicely dressed," he said, scanning Frank's appearance critically. "I guess you must be prospering."

"I am doing very well, Pliny," answered Frank, smiling.

"And you pay your board, too—and washing?"

"I earn enough for all my expenses."

"Then you must get more'n four dollars a week."

"I don't think I could get along very well on four dollars a week."

"That's all I get. I ought to be raised, but my boss won't pay me a cent more. He's awful mean."

"It seems to me you are unlucky."

"So I am. I should like to come to New York to work. What are you doing?"

"I am private secretary to a gentleman living on Madison Avenue."

Pliny opened his eyes in genuine surprise.

"Private secretary! What do you do?"

"I read to him, write his letters, and I also give lessons to his little grandson."

"You don't say!" ejaculated Pliny, in astonishment. "How much do you get?"

"Fifty dollars a month and my board," replied Frank, enjoying Pliny's surprise.

"You don't mean it!" exclaimed Pliny, opening wide his eyes in bewildered surprise.

"Certainly I mean it."

"Why, that's about twelve dollars a week, and board besides."

"Yes."

"Do you have to work hard?"

"Not very. I have several hours a day to myself."

"I never heard of such a thing!" ejaculated Pliny. "You're awfully lucky. How did you get it?"

"It's too long a story to tell, Pliny."

"Do you think I could get a place like that?" asked Pliny, anxiously. "I'd be willing to work cheaper than that."

"I don't think such chances are very common," said Frank, gravely.

"How old are you?" asked Pliny, abruptly.

"Sixteen."

"Just my age, and I'm working for four dollars a week," said Pliny, looking unhappy and discontented.

"I don't think you could get any higher wages in New York in the same kind of a store. I didn't try to get a place, because I couldn't support myself on a boy's wages."

"What did you do before you got to be private secretary?"

"I was for a few weeks agent for a large tea company."

"Did it pay well?"

"No. I couldn't make enough to pay expenses."

"How long have you been in this place?"

"Nearly six months."

"You must have saved up considerable money," suggested Pliny.

"I have saved up something."

Pliny became interested.

"How much?"

"I don't care to mention."

"Oh, I didn't suppose it was a secret. Will you lend me five dollars?"

"No!" answered Frank, decidedly.

"I should think you might," said Pliny, complainingly.

"I see no reason why I should. You have a good home, and enough to provide for all your wants."

"You are a good deal better off."

'I may lose my position, and then I must live on what I have saved till I can get something else to do. You ought not to stand in need of money."

Pliny had seventy-five dollars in a bank at Newark, but it struck him that it would be a good plan to borrow five dollars from Frank and add to his account. He would not have dreamed of repaying the money. He was essentially a mean boy, and considered all his friends and acquaintances who had money legitimate prey.

"I haven't had any lunch," he said to Frank, changing his form of attack.

"Shall I show you a restaurant?"

"No; I guess I will get along till I get home. I've had to pay out more for clothes than I expected, and then it's expensive paying railroad fares."

Frank understood very well what Pliny meant, and said, with a smile:

"Won't you come and lunch with me, Pliny?

I can't invite you to the house, because that would be a liberty; but I will take you to a restaurant near by, and shall be glad to have you order what you like."

"I don't mind if I do," said Pliny, with alacrity. "You're a good fellow, Frank, and I'm glad you're getting on so well. Father said he didn't believe you'd make out in the city, but I thought different. He thought you wanted to stay in Newark, and live at our house, considering you had lost your property."

"I hope he has changed his mind about that," said Frank, feeling annoyed at the meanness of his relative.

"He will, when he hears what a good place you've got. You see, father's been expecting you would get hard up, and write him for money."

"Would he have sent me any?"

"I guess not. It's as hard to get money out of father as—as anything. He ought not to make me buy my clothes. I leave it to you if he had."

"I would rather not express any opinion about that," said Frank. "You may say to your father, when you get home, that he need not have been afraid of my applying to him for money. Once I got nearly out of money, but I never even thought of him."

"Yes, I'll tell him. I guess he'll invite you to come out and spend Sunday, when he hears how well you are getting along."

Frank did not reply, but he privately decided that such a visit would offer no attractions to him. He would rather remain in New York.

"I hope I never shall think so much of money as Pliny and his father," thought Frank. "Money is a good thing to have, but there are some things that are better."

Pliny did justice to his cousin's hospitality. Accustomed to his father's meager table, he enjoyed highly the restaurant dinner, and was by no means bashful in ordering. Frank was pleased to see how Pliny enjoyed the meal. In fact, he sympathized with him, knowing the plainness of his father's table.

Soon after they parted.

"I hope I'll see you when I come to York again, Cousin Frank," said Pliny.

"Thank you! It will give me pleasure to have you lunch with me again, whenever we meet."

CHAPTER XXXVII.

A LETTER FROM MR. TARBOX.

FRANK did not speak to Mr. Percival's family of his meeting with Pliny. It was not pleasant to him to think that he was valued only for his good fortune. He had seen but little of the Tarbox family, but he understood very well what their professions of friendship amounted to, and they were not to be relied upon in an emergency.

He was not much surprised on Monday afternoon to receive the following letter from Erastus Tarbox:

"MY DEAR YOUNG COUSIN:—We have been wondering what has become of you, and Mrs. T. and myself have often wished to invite you to pass a Sabbath at our humble home. Not knowing your address, I could not write to you, or I should have done so. You can imagine, therefore, the pleasure we felt when Pliny told us that he had met you, and gave us tidings of your remarkable success, which I am sure does you great credit.

"He tells me that you fill a very responsible position, and receive a very liberal salary. I could wish that Pliny might be equally fortunate, and shall esteem it a great favor if you will mention him to your respected employer, and recommend him for any lucrative position which he may bestow upon him. Pliny is a very capable boy, and has been carefully trained to habits of frugality and industry.

"Can you not soon come out and pass a Sabbath with us? The esteem which we have for your late lamented mother alone would secure you a cordial welcome, not to speak of our friendship for yourself. Pliny often says that you seem to him like a brother, and he would truly enjoy your companionship.

"Your sincere friend and cousin,

"ERASTUS TARBOX."

The time was when Frank would have put

confidence in the friendly expressions used by Mr. Tarbox, but his eyes had been opened, and he understood that if misfortune should come to him, it would not do to lean upon his cousins at Newark.

Frank wrote a civil reply to Mr. Tarbox, thanking him for his invitation, but saying that at present it would not be convenient for him to accept it. He added that should an opportunity offer he would be glad to assist Pliny to a better position than he now held.

In spite of his wish to be cordial, his letter was felt by the Tarbox family to be cold, and they regretted that they had not treated him better during his brief visit to them.

But then how could they suppose he would be so successful? If the time should ever come when he recovered his property, they would be prepared to make a determined effort to convinced him that they had always been his affectionate friends.

About this time Frank received another letter, which afforded him greater satisfaction than the one from Newark.

This letter was from Col. Vincent, who, it will be remembered, had purchased Ajax when Mr. Manning persisted in selling him. It was as follows:

"My Dear Frank: I learned incidentally from one of our townsmen, who recently met you in New York, that you have been very successful in obtaining employment, and that of an honorable and responsible character. It relieved my mind, for, knowing how hard it is for a boy to make his own way in a large city, I feared that you might be suffering privation, or living poorly. I hope, however, you would in that case have applied to me for such help as your father's old friend would have been glad to offer.

"Your stepfather has not been heard from directly. I learn, however, from some friends who have met him abroad that he is having trouble with Mark, who is proving difficult to manage, and has contracted a dangerous taste for gaming. Mr. Manning was obliged to leave Baden-Baden on account of this unfortunate tendency, and is even thinking of returning to the Cedars, where his son will be removed from temptation. To this, however, Mark will be likely to make strenuous opposition. He will find it dull to settle down here after having tasted the gayety of Europe."

Here followed a little local gossip, which the writer thought might prove interesting to Frank, and the letter concluded with a cordial invitation to our hero to spend a Sunday with him, or a longer time, if he could be spared from his duties.

Frank was disposed to accept the invitation, but his acceptance was postponed by an unusual service which he was called upon to render to Mr. Percival.

Of this the reader will hear everything in the next chapter.

CHAPTER XXXVIII.

MR. PERCIVAL'S PROPOSAL.

ONE morning, after writing several letters for his employer, the young secretary asked Mr. Percival if he had any further commands.

The old gentleman answered thoughtfully:

"I have been thinking of asking you to do me an unusual service."

"I shall be very glad to serve you in any way, Mr. Percival," said Frank, promptly.

"I have no doubt of it," said the old gentleman, kindly. "I have observed your willingness to undertake any duty, and, still more, your disposition to perform it thoroughly. In this particular case, however, I have been considering whether a boy of your age would be competent to do what I desire."

Frank was not self-distrustful, neither was he overconfident. He was naturally energetic and ambitious to distinguish himself, and not afraid to undertake any difficult task.

"Will you try me, Mr. Percival?" he said. "I will do my best to succeed."

"I am quite inclined to try you, Frank," said Mr. Percival; "the more so because I know of no one else in whom I could confide. But I must give you an idea of what I have in view. It would require you to make a journey."

Frank listened to this gladly. To a boy of

his age, who had seen but little of the world, a journey offered attractions.

"I should like to travel," he said.

"I have no doubt about that," said Mr. Percival, smiling. "At your age I am sure I should have been equally willing to see something of the world, though traveling involved at that time far more hardships than at present. Now, however, I like best to stay by the fireside, and should dread very much a journey to Minnesota."

"To Minnesota!" exclaimed Frank, with sparkling eyes.

He had not thought of a journey so extended.

"Yes; it would be necessary for you to go out to Minnesota. Ordinarily, a man can best look after his own affairs; but in the present instance, I suspect that you could do better than myself. I don't mean this as a compliment, but a boy like you would not be suspected, and so could discover more than I, from whom facts would be studiously concealed. But, of course, you don't understand my meaning. I will explain, and then you can comprehend me."

Frank was all attention.

"You must know that I own a good deal of property in a certain township in Southern Minnesota. When a young man, I bought three hundred and twenty acres of land in the township of Jackson, obtaining it at a slight advance on government rates.

"Some improvements had been made, and I was induced to visit the place. I found but three families in residence, but I saw also that the place had large natural advantages, water-power, etc., and presented an unusually favorable site for a village. I had considerable means, and started the village by erecting a dozen houses, a store, a sawmill, gristmill, and so on.

"This formed a nucleus, and soon quite a village sprang up. The sawmill and gristmill proved profitable, all my houses were tenanted, and I erected more, securing also additional land. In course of time I was induced to sell some of my houses, but I still own two stores, a dozen houses, the saw and gristmills, besides two outlying farms.

"Living so far away, I could not attend personally to the business connected with my investment, and was compelled to appoint an agent. Up to four years since, I was fortunate enough to possess the services of a capable and trustworthy man, named Sampson. He died after a few weeks' illness, and I was compelled to look out for a successor.

"Now, I had a distant cousin, who had never succeeded very well in life, and was at that time seeking for employment of some kind. He heard of the vacancy, and importuned me to appoint him as my agent in Jackson. I had no reason to doubt his honesty, though his repeated failures might well have led me to suspect his capacity. I was weak enough, as I now consider it, to yield to his importunities and give him the post he sought.

"The result was that durng the first year of his incumbency the amount turned over to me was only three-fourths as much as in the last year of his predecessor. The second year there was a further falling off. The same happened the third year, until at the present time my rents amount to less than half what they were in Mr. Sampson's time.

"Of course, my suspicions that my cousin was at least inefficient were aroused long since. I have repeatedly asked an explanation of the diminished revenues, and plenty of excuses have been made, but they do not seem to me satisfactory.

"Moreover, I have heard a rumor that Mr. Fairfield is intemperate in his habits, and I have considerable reason to believe that the story is correct. I have made up my mind that something must be done. A regard for my own interests requires that if any agent is unfaithful he should be displaced, and I wish to find out from some reliable source the true state of the case.

"Now I will tell you what I have in view. I propose to send you out to Jackson to investigate and report to me your impressions of the manner in which Mr. Fairfield discharges his duties, and whether you think a change should be made in the agency."

Frank listened to Mr. Percival with a flushed

face and a feeling of gratification and pride that he should be thought of in connection with a responsible duty.

"I am very much obliged to you, Mr. Percival," he said, "for thinking of me in such a connection. You may feel that I am presumptuous for thinking I have any chance of successfully accomplishing what you desire, but if you are willing to trust me, I am willing to undertake it, and by following your instructions closely, and doing my best, I think I can succeed."

"I am willing to trust you, Frank," said Mr. Percival. "You are a boy, to be sure, but you have unusually good judgment, and I know you will be faithful to my interests. I understand, then, that you are willing to go out as my accredited representative?"

"Yes, sir. When do you want me to start?" said Frank, promptly.

"As soon as you can get ready."

"I will start to-morrow, if you desire it, sir."

"Let it be to-morrow, then. We will now discuss some of the details connected with the mission."

CHAPTER XXXIX.

PREPARING FOR A JOURNEY.

After receiving certain instructions from Mr. Percival in regard to the manner of carrying on his inquiries, Frank said:

"There is one thing I have thought of, Mr. Percival, that may interfere with my success."

"What is it, Frank? I shall be glad to receive any suggestion from you."

"I have been thinking, sir, that it may excite surprise that I should come to Jackson, and remain there without any apparent motive. Perhaps Mr. Fairfield might suspect that I came from you."

"I hardly think so, Frank. He would not suppose that I would select so young a messenger. Still, it will be well to think of some pretext for your stay. Can you help me?"

"I have been thinking, sir, that I might fit myself out as an agent, or peddler, or something of the kind. It would not only give me an excuse for my journey, but enable me to call from house to house and pick up information about Mr. Fairfield."

"A capital idea, Frank. I see that you are better fitted for the task than I supposed. I give you authority to fit yourself out in any way you choose. I shall have to leave a great deal to your own judgment."

"Then, sir, I think I might lay in a stock of stationery, pens and articles of that nature. Probably this is so common that I would be thought to be nothing more than I seemed."

"That strikes me rather favorably, Frank."

"I could fit myself out in the city, and take the articles along with me in an extra valise or carpet-bag."

"Let me suggest an amendment to your plan," said Mr. Percival. "Wait till you get to Chicago, and lay in your stock there. The advantage of that arrangement will be that you will be saved the care of your merchandise up to that point, and, as you may be asked where you obtained your stock, it will create less surprise if you mention Chicago than New York. It would be considered hardly worth while for a New York boy to go so far on such a business trip."

This seemed to Frank an excellent suggestion and he instantly adopted it.

The next day Frank started on his long journey. He carried with him a supply of money provided by Mr. Percival, and he was authorized to draw for more if he should require it.

He divided this money into two portions, keeping a small sum in his pocketbook, but the greater part of it in an inside vest pocket, where it would not be likely to be looked for by pickpockets.

This arrangement was suggested by Mr. Percival.

"I once experienced," he said, "the disadvantage of carrying all my money in one pocket. I was in a Southern city, or, rather, on my way to it, when an adroit pickpocket on the car relieved me of my wallet containing all my available funds. I did not find out my loss till I had arrived at the hotel and registered my name. You can imagine my embarrassment. It was my first visit to that particular city, and I had no acquaintances there, so far as I was aware. Had I mentioned my position to the landlord, he might very probably have taken me for an adventurer, traveling on false pretenses."

"What did you do, sir?" asked Frank, interested.

"I took a walk about the city, my thoughts occupied in devising a way out of my trouble. To my great relief, I had the good fortune, during the walk, to meet a New York acquaintance, who knew very well my financial standing. I told him of my difficulty, and he immediately introduced me at a bank, where I raised money on a New York draft. I resolved, however, at that time, never again to carry all my money in one pocketbook, as boats and railroad trains on the long routes are generally infested by pickpockets and sharpers."

Frank at once set about preparing for his journey.

He bought a ready-made suit of blue cloth, not unlike that worn by the district telegraph boys of to-day, which he judged would look more suitable than his ordinary attire for the character he was about to assume of a traveling peddler.

He bought a through ticket to the railroad point nearest Jackson, and then, bidding good-by to Mr. Percival and his family, started on his trip.

Little Freddie made strenuous opposition to parting with his favorite, but Frank promised to bring him home a present, and this diverted the little fellow's thoughts.

CHAPTER XL.

FRANK REACHES JACKSON.

It was four o'clock in the afternoon when Frank Courtney left the cars and set foot on the platform before the station at Prescott, five miles distant from the town of Jackson, in Southern Minnesota.

He looked about him, but could see no village.

Prescott was a stopping place for the cars, but there was no settlement of any account there, as he afterward found.

He had supposed he would find a stage in waiting to convey him to Jackson, but it was clear that the business was not large enough to warrant such a conveyance.

Looking about him, Frank saw a farm wagon, the driver of which had evidently come to receive some freight which had come by rail.

Approaching the driver, who seemed to be—though roughly dressed—an intelligent man, Frank inquired:

"How far is Jackson from here, sir?"

"Five miles," was the answer.

"Is there any stage running there from this depot?"

"Oh, no! If there were, it wouldn't average two passengers a day."

"Then I suppose I must walk," said Frank, looking rather doubtfully at the two heavy valises which constituted his baggage.

"Then you are going to Jackson?"

"Yes, sir."

"I come from Jackson myself, and in fifteen minutes shall start on my way back. You may ride and welcome."

"Thank you, sir!" said our hero, quite relieved. "I hope you will allow me to pay you as much as I should have to pay in a stage."

'No, no, my lad," said the farmer, heartily. "The horse can draw you as well as not, and I shall be glad to have your company."

"Thank you, sir!"

"Just climb up here, then. I'll take your baggage and put it on the wagon behind."

When the farmer had loaded up, he started up the team. Then, finding himself at leisure, he proceeded to satisfy his curiosity by cross-examining his young passenger.

"Do you come from the East?" he asked.

"I am last from Chicago," answered Frank, cautiously.

"I suppose you ve got some friends in Jackson?" ventured the farmer, interrogatively.

Frank smiled.

"You are the only man living in Jackson that I ever met," he said.

"Indeed!" said the driver, puzzled. "Are you calculating to make a long stay in our village?" he asked again, after a minute's pause.

"That depends on business," answered the young traveler.

"Are you in business?"

"I have a stock of stationery which I shall offer for sale in Jackson," answered Frank.

"I am afraid you'll find it rather a poor market. If that's all you have to depend upon, I am afraid you'll get discouraged."

"I am also agent for an illustrated book," said Frank. "I may be able to dispose of a few."

"Perhaps so," answered the farmer, dubiously. "But our people haven't much money to spend on articles of luxury, and books are a luxury with us."

"I always heard that Jackson was a flourishing place," said Frank, who felt that now was his time to obtain a little information.

"It ought to be," said the farmer; "but there's one thing prevents."

"What is that?"

"A good deal of our village is owned by a New York man, to whom we have to pay rent. He has a rascally agent—a Mr. Fairfield—who grinds us down by his exactions, and does what he can to keep us in debt."

"Has he always been agent?"

"No. Before he came there was an excellent man—a Mr. Sampson—who treated us fairly, contented himself with exacting rents which we could pay, and if a man were unlucky, would wait a reasonable time for him to pay. Then we got along comfortably. But he died, and this man was sent out in his place. Then commenced a new state of things. He immediately raised the rents, demanded that they should be paid on the day they were due, and made himself harsh and tyrannical."

"Do you think the man who employs him knows how he is conducting his agency?" Frank inquired.

"No; there is no one to tell him. I suppose Mr. Fairfield tells him a smooth story, and he believes it. I am afraid we can hope for no relief."

"What would he say," thought Frank, "if he knew I were a messenger from Mr. Percival?"

"What sort of a man is this Mr. Fairfield in private life?" he asked.

"He drinks like a fish," was the unexpected reply. "Frequently he appears on the street under the influence of liquor. He spends a good deal of money, lives in a large house, and his wife dresses expensively. He must get a much larger salary than Mr. Sampson did, or he could not spend money as he does."

Though Frank had not much worldly experience, he could not help coming to the conclusion that Mr. Fairfield was acting dishonestly.

He put together the two circumstances that this new agent had increased the rents, and yet that he had returned to Mr. Percival only about half as much as his predecessor had done. Clearly, he must retain in his own hands much more than he had a right to do.

"I shall have to report unfavorably on this man," he thought.

One point must be considered—where he was to find a boarding-place on his arrival in Jackson.

"Is there a hotel in Jackson?" he asked.

"There is a tavern, but it's a low place," answered the farmer. "A good deal of liquor is sold there, and Mr. Fairfield, our agent, is one of the most constant patrons of the bar."

"I don't think I should like to stop there," said Frank. "Isn't there any private family where I can get board for a week or two?"

"If you don't object to plain fare," said the farmer, "I might agree to board you myself."

This was precisely what Frank wanted, and he replied that nothing would suit him better.

"We live humbly," continued Mr. Hamlin—for this, Frank learned, was his driver's name—"but we will try to make you comfortable."

"I feel sure of that, sir, and I am much obliged to you for receiving me."

"As to terms, you can pay whatever you can afford. My wife and children will be glad to see you. It's pretty quiet out here, and it breaks the monotony to meet any person from the East."

"How long have you lived in Jackson, Mr. Hamlin?"

"About eight years. I was not brought up as a farmer, but became one from necessity. I was a bookkeeper in Chicago for a good many years, until I found the confinement and close work were injuring my health. Then I came here and set up as a farmer. I got along pretty well, at first; at any rate, I made a living for my family; but when Mr. Fairfield became agent, he raised my rent, and, in other ways, made it hard for me. Now I have a hard struggle."

"I thought you were not always a farmer," said Frank.

"What made you think so?"

"You don't talk like a farmer. You have the appearance of a man who has lived in cities."

"Seems to me you are a close observer, for a boy of your years," said Mr. Hamlin, shrewdly.

Frank smiled.

"I should be glad if your compliment were deserved," he answered. "It's a pity you were not agent, instead of Mr. Fairfield," suggested Frank, pointedly.

"I wish I were," answered Hamlin. "I believe I should make a good one, though I might not turn over as much money to my employer. I should, first of all, lower the rents and make it as easy for the tenants as I could in justice to my New York principal."

"Do you know how much Mr. Fairfield receives—how large a salary, I mean?"

"I know what Mr. Sampson got—twelve hundred dollars a year; but Mr. Fairfield lives at the rate of more than twice that sum, if I can judge from appearances."

"I suppose you would be contented with the salary which Mr. Sampson received?"

"Contented! I should feel like a rich man. It would not interfere with my carrying on my farm, and I should be able to make something from that. Why, it is as much as I received as a bookkeeper, and here the expenses of living are small, compared with what they were in Chicago. I could save money and educate my children, as I cannot do now. I have a boy who wants a classical education, but of course there are no schools here which can afford it, and I am too poor to send him away from home. I suppose I shall have to bring him up as a farmer, though it is a great pity, for he is not fitted for it."

Mr. Hamlin sighed, but Frank felt in unusually good spirits. He saw his way clear already, not only to recommend Mr. Fairfield's displacement, but to urge Mr. Hamlin's appointment in his stead; that is, if his favorable impressions were confirmed on further acquaintance.

"It seems to me," said the driver, changing the subject, "you might find something better to do than to peddle stationery."

"I don't mean to follow the business long," answered Frank.

"It can't pay you much."

"I am not wholly dependent upon it," said our hero. "There is one advantage about it. It enables me to travel about and pay my expenses, and you know traveling is agreeable to a boy of my age."

"That is true. Well, your expenses won't amount to much while you are in Jackson. I shall only charge you just enough to cover expenses—say three dollars a week."

Frank was about to insist on paying a larger sum, but it occurred to him that he must keep up appearances, and he therefore only thanked his kind acquaintance.

By this time they had entered the village of Jackson.

"There's Mr. Fairfield now!" said Mr. Hamlin, suddenly, pointing with his whip to a rather tall, stout man, with a red nose and inflamed countenance, who was walking unsteadily along the sidewalk.

Frank carefully scrutinized the agent, and mentally decided that such a man was unfit for the responsible position he held.

CHAPTER XLI.

DICK HAMLIN.

Mr. Hamlin stopped his horse a quarter of a mile from the village in front of a plain farmhouse.

An intelligent-looking boy, of perhaps fifteen, coarsely but neatly dressed, approached and greeted his father, not without a glance of surprise and curiosity at Frank.

"You may unharness the horses, Dick," said Mr. Hamlin. "When you come back, I will introduce you to a boy friend who will stay with us a while."

Dick obeyed, and Frank followed his host into the house.

Here he was introduced to Mrs. Hamlin, a motherly-looking woman, and Annie and Grace, younger sisters of Dick.

"I am glad to see you," said Mrs. Hamlin, to our hero, after a brief explanation from her husband. "We will try to make you comfortable."

"Thank you!" said Frank. "I am sure I shall feel at home."

The house was better furnished than might have been anticipated. When Mr. Hamlin left Chicago, he had some money saved up, and he furnished his house in a comfortable manner.

It was not, however, the furniture that attracted Frank's attention so much as the books, papers and pictures that gave the rooms a homelike appearance.

"I shall be much better off here than I would have been at the tavern," he thought. "This seems like home."

"I see," said Mr. Hamlin, "that you are surprised to see so many books and pictures. I admit that my house does not look like the house of a poor man, who has to struggle for the mere necessaries of life. But books and periodicals we have always classed among the necessities, and I am sure we would all rather limit ourselves to dry bread for two out of the three meals than to give up this food for the mind."

"I think you are a very sensible man, Mr. Hamlin," said Frank. "I couldn't get along without something to read."

"Not in this out-of-the-way place, at any rate," said Mr. Hamlin. "Nothing can be more dismal than the homes of some of my neighbors, who spend as much, or more, than I do every year. Yet, they consider me extravagant because I buy books and subscribe for periodicals."

By this time, Dick came in from the barn.

"Dick," said his father, "this is Frank Courtney, who comes from Chicago on a business errand. He is a traveling merchant——"

"In other words, a peddler," said Frank, with a smile, "ready to give the good people in Jackson a chance to buy stationery at reasonable prices."

"He will board with us while he is canvassing the neighborhood, and I expect you and he will become great friends."

"I think we shall," said Frank.

Dick was a little shy, but a few minutes set him quite at his ease with his new acquaintance.

After supper, Frank said:

"Dick, if you are at leisure, I wish you would take a walk about the village with me. I want to see how it looks."

"All right," said Dick.

When the two left the house, the country boy began to ask questions.

"How do you like your business?" he asked.

"Not very well," answered Frank. "I do not think I shall stay in it very long."

"Do you sell enough to make your expenses?" asked Dick.

"No; but I am not wholly dependent on my sales. I have a little income—a hundred dollars a year—paid me by my stepfather."

"I wish I had as much. It seems a good deal to me."

"It doesn't go very far. What are you intending to be, Dick?"

"I suppose I shall have to be a farmer, though I don't like it."

"What would you like to be?"

'I should like to get an education," said Dick, his eyes lighting up. "I should like to study Latin and Greek, and go to college. Then I could be a teacher or a lawyer. But there is no chance of that," he added, his voice falling.

"Don't be too sure of that, Dick," said Frank, hopefully. "Something may turn up in your favor."

"Nothing ever does turn up in Jackson,"

said the boy, in a tone of discouragement. "Father is a poor man, and has hard work to get along. He can give me no help."

"Isn't the farm productive?"

"There is no trouble about that, but he has to pay too high a rent. It's all the fault of Fairfield."

"The agent?"

"Yes."

"Your father was telling me about him. Now, if your father were in his place, I suppose he could give you the advantages you wish."

"Oh, yes! There would be no trouble then. I am sure he would make a better and more popular agent than Mr. Fairfield; but there is no use thinking about that."

"I expected myself to go to college," said Frank. "In fact, I have studied Latin and Greek, and in less than a year I could be ready to enter."

"Why don't you?" asked Dick.

"You forget that I am a poor peddler"

"Then how were you able to get so good an education?" asked Dick, in surprise.

"Because I was once better off than I am now. The fact is, Dick," he added, "I have seen better days. But when I was reduced to poverty, I gave up hopes of a college education and became what I am."

"Wasn't it hard?"

"Not so much as you might suppose. My

home was not happy. I have a stepfather and stepbrother, neither of whom I like. In fact, there is no love lost between us. I was not obliged to leave home, but under the circumstances I preferred to."

"Where are your stepfather and your stepbrother now?"

"They are traveling in Europe."

"While you are working hard for a living! That does not seem to be just."

"We must make the best of circumstances, Dick. Whose is that large house on the left?"

"That belongs to Mr. Fairfield."

"He seems to live nicely."

"Yes, he has improved and enlarged the house a good deal since he moved into it—at Mr. Percival's expense, I suppose."

"He seems to have pretty much his own way here," said Frank.

"Yes. Mr. Percival never comes to Jackson, and I suppose he believes all that the agent tells him."

"He may get found out some time."

"I wish he might. It would be a great blessing to Jackson if he were removed and a good man were put in his place."

"That may happen some day."

"Not very likely, I am afraid."

At this moment Mr. Fairfield himself came out of his front gate.

"Hello, Hamlin!" he said, roughly, to Dick. "Is your father at home?"

"Yes, sir."

"I have something to say to him. I think I will call round."

"You will find him at home, sir."

"Dick," said Frank, when the agent had passed on, "do you mind going back? What you tell me makes me rather curious about Mr. Fairfield. At your house I may get a chance to see something of him."

"Let us go back, then," said Dick; "but I don't think, Frank, that you will care much about keeping up the acquaintance."

"Perhaps not; but I shall gratify my curiosity."

The two boys turned and followed the agent closely. They reached the house about five minutes after Mr. Fairfield.

CHAPTER XLII.

MR. FAIRFIELD, THE AGENT.

THE two boys found Mr. Fairfield already seated in the most comfortable chair in the sitting-room.

He looked inquiringly at Frank when he entered with Dick.

"Who is that boy, Hamlin?" inquired the agent. "Nephew of yours?"

"No, sir. It is a young man who has come to Jackson on business."

"What kind of business?"

"I sell stationery," Frank answered for himself.

"Oh, a peddler!" said the agent, contemptuously.

"Many of our most successful men began in that way," said Mr. Hamlin, fearing lest Frank's feelings might be hurt.

"I never encourage peddlers myself," said Mr. Fairfield, pompously.

"Then I suppose it will be of no use for me to call at your door," said Frank, who, in place of being mortified, was amused by the agent's arrogance.

"I should say not, unless your back is proof against a broomstick," answered Fairfield, coarsely. "I tell my servant to treat all who call in that way."

"I won't put her to the trouble of using it," said Frank, disgusted at the man's ill manners.

"That's where you are wise—yes, wise and prudent—young man."

Mr. Fairfield was far from supposing that the boy whom he considered so insignificant was sitting in judgment upon him, and even held his fate in his hands. The idea would have seemed to him the wildest absurdity. Had he really believed it, however, he would have been as obsequious as he was insolent.

"And now, Hamlin," said the agent, "I may as well come to business."

"To business!" repeated the farmer, rather surprised, for there was no rent due for a month to come.

"Yes, to business," said Fairfield. "I came to give you notice that after the next payment I shall feel obliged to raise your rent."

"Raise my rent!" exclaimed the farmer, in genuine dismay. "I am already paying a considerably higher rent than I paid to your predecessor."

"Can't help it. Old Sampson was a slow-going old fogy. He didn t do his duty by his employer. When I came in, I turned over a new leaf."

"You certainly did," the farmer could not help saying, bitterly.

"What do you mean by that, eh?" asked the agent, suspiciously.

"I mean to agree with you, sir."

"I suppose you liked old Sampson better than you do me?"

"I certainly got along better in his time."

"No doubt. He was a great deal too easy with you. Didn't do his duty, sir. Wasn't sharp enough. That's all."

"You certainly cannot be in earnest in raising my rent, Mr. Fairfield," said the farmer, uneasily.

"I certainly am."

"I can hardly get along as it is. I find it hard to make both ends meet."

"Of course I expected to hear you say that, but it's all bosh," said the agent, coarsely. "Why, I need only to look around me to see signs of luxury—books, magazines, pictures, nice furniture. Come, Hamlin, that won't do. There's no one in Jackson, except myself, that can show such a sitting-room as this."

"If you allude to the pictures and furniture, I brought them with me. As to the papers and books, we economize in every other direction in order to afford these. Living out of the world, as we do, we can't get along very well without them."

"Just so; only you are not living like the poor man you pretend to be."

"I can't live at all if you increase my rent, which is already larger than I can afford to pay, Mr. Fairfield."

"Oh, I won't raise it much—say ten dollars a quarter."

"I can't pay it."

"Then I must find a tenant who can and will," said the agent, empathcially.

"In other words, you mean to turn me out, Mr. Fairfield?"

"Only if you won't pay your rent. That is fair, is it not?"

"The rent is very unfair. You are a very hard man, Mr. Fairfield."

"You forget, Hamlin, that I am only an agent. Mr. Percival writes me that he doesn't receive enough income from his property out here. Well, of course, I have to obey his orders. The only way to get a larger increase is to raise the rents, don't you see?"

"Is there to be a general raise, Mr. Fairfield?"

"Yes. You are the first one I've come to, but I shall see the rest."

"Then I am sorry for my neighbors. They are no better able to pay a larger rent than I am."

"Oh, they'll agree to it when they find they have to," said Fairfield, carelessly.

"I am sure Mr. Percival can't understand the true state of the case, or the circumstances of his tenants. Will you give me his address, and I will take the liberty of writing to him and respectfully remonstrate against any increase?"

Mr. Fairfield looked uneasy.

This appeal would not at all suit him. Yet how could he object without leading to the suspicion that he was acting in this matter wholly on his own responsibility, and not by the express orders of his principal? How could he refuse to furnish Mr. Percival's address?

A middle course occurred to him.

"You may write your appeal if you like, Hamlin," he said, "and hand it to me. I will forward it; though I don't believe it will do any good. The fact is that Mr. Percival has made up his mind to have more income from his property in Jackson."

"He never troubled us when Mr. Sampson was agent. though we paid smaller rents than we do now."

"Very likely; but he was better off then.

He has been losing money by bad investments lately, and this leads him to put on the screws here."

There was no truth in this story, as may readily be believed. It was the invention of the moment, and struck Mr. Fairfield as very clever. For truth he cared little or nothing, providing he could further his own designs.

The agent had said what he came to say, and took his leave.

Mr. Hamlin was depressed by his visit.

"I don't see what I am to do," he said to his wife. "It is only by the greatest effort that I can pay my present rent, and to pay forty dollars a year more is simply impossible."

"Won't Mr. Fairfield relent?" asked his wife.

"Not he. He will exact the last dollar of his demand."

"Mr. Hamlin," said Frank, "don't be discouraged. Better times may be nearer than you suppose."

"I wish I could think so."

"At any rate, hope for the best."

"I will, if I can."

That evening Frank wrote a long letter to Mr. Percival, communicating the information he had already obtained as to the character and methods of his agent.

He had been in Jackson only a few hours, but he felt that he had already discovered enough to condemn the unfaithful steward.

This letter he mailed the very first thing on the following morning, and then quietly awaited an answer. It might be a week before he could receive a reply to his letter.

CHAPTER XLIII.

FRANK RECEIVES A LETTER FROM MR. PERCIVAL.

WHILE Frank was waiting for an answer to his letter, he devoted a part of this time daily to the business which was supposed to be his only reason for remaining in Jackson.

I am bound to say that as regards this business his trip might be pronounced a failure. There was little ready money in Jackson. Many of the people were tenants of Mr. Percival, and found it difficult to pay the excessive rents demanded by his agent. Of course, they had no money to spare for extras. Even if they had been better off, there was little demand for stationery in the village. The people were chiefly farmers, and did not indulge in much correspondence.

When Frank returned to his boarding place on the afternoon of the first day, Mr. Hamlin asked him, not without solicitude, with what luck he had met.

"I have sold twenty-five cents' worth of note paper," answered Frank, with a smile.

Mr. Hamlin looked troubled.

"How many places did you call at?" he inquired.

"About a dozen."

"I am afraid you will get discouraged."

"I am not easily discouraged, Mr. Hamlin."

"If you don't do better, you won't begin to pay expenses."

"That is true."

"But perhaps you may do better to-morrow."

"I hope so."

The next day Frank succeeded in making sales to the amount of thirty-two cents, and so reported to his host.

"I am afraid you won't care to remain long in Jackson," said the farmer, with whom, as well as his family, our hero had already become a favorite.

"I think I shall remain a fortnight," answered Frank, "whatever luck I meet with. I have done much better for some time past; and can afford to give myself a little rest."

"I am glad you don't feel troubled by your poor success, Frank."

"You make me feel so much at home," said Frank, "that I don't care much for a short time how my business prospers."

"I wish you could find something in Jackson that would induce you to remain here permanently, and make your home with us. I would charge you only the bare cost of board."

"Thank you very much, Mr. Hamlin. I should enjoy being with you, but I don't believe

I shall find any opening here. Besides, I like a more stirring life."

"No doubt—no doubt! Boys like a lively place. Well, I am glad you feel independent of your business."

"For a little time. I am afraid it wouldn't do for me to earn so little for any length of time."

Frank enjoyed the society of Dick Hamlin. Together they went fishing and hunting, and a mutual liking sprang up between them.

"I wish you were going to stay longer, Frank," said Dick. "I shall feel lonely when you are gone."

"We may meet again under different circumstances," said Frank. "While I am here, we will enjoy ourselves as well as we can."

So the days passed, and at length a letter came from Mr. Percival. I append the most important passages:

"Your report is clear, and I have perfect confidence in your statement. Mr. Fairfield has abused my confidence and oppressed my tenants, and I shall dismiss him. I am glad you have found in Jackson a man who is capable of succeeding him. Solely upon your recommendation, I shall appoint Mr. Hamlin my resident agent and representative for the term of six months. Should he acquit himself to my satisfaction, he will be continued in the position. I am prepared to offer him one hundred dollars a month, if that will content him.

"Upon receipt of this letter, and the accompanying legal authority, you may call upon Mr. Fairfield and require him to transfer his office, and the papers and accounts connected with it, to Mr. Hamlin. I inclose a check for three hundred dollars, payable to your order, which you may make payable to him. in lieu of three months' notice, provided he immediately surrenders his office. Should he not, I shall dismiss him summarily, and proceed against him for the moneys he has misappropriated to his own use, and you may so inform him."

With this letter was a letter to Mr. Fairfield, of the same purport, and a paper appointing Mr. Hamlin agent.

When this letter was received, Frank was overjoyed, knowing how much pleasure he was about to give his new friends.

With this appointment and salary, Mr. Hamlin would consider himself a rich man, and Dick's hope for a liberal education might be realized.

The letter came just before supper, and, at the close of the evening meal, Frank determined to inform his friends of their good fortune.

"Mr. Hamlin," said he, "I have some good news for you."

"Indeed!" said the farmer, surprised.

"Your rent will not be increased."

"But how do you know this? Has Mr. Fairfield told you so?"

"No," answered Frank. "I have a question to ask. Would you be willing to take Mr. Fairfield's place at a hundred dollars a month?"

"Willing? I should be delighted to do so. But why do you say this?"

"Because," answered Frank, quietly, "I am authorized to offer it to you at that salary."

The whole family looked at Frank in bewildered surprise. It occurred to them that he might have become crazy.

"You!" exclaimed the farmer. "What can you have to do with the agency?"

"I came to Jackson," answered Frank, quietly, "at the request of Mr. Percival, and as his representative. You are surprised that he should select a young peddler, but I came here in that capacity only to avoid suspicion. I am Mr. Percival's private secretary when in New York, and he had sufficient confidence in me to send me here to make an examination and report. I have recommended your appointment as agent, and he authorized me to offer it to you."

"I can hardly believe my ears," said the farmer, amazement struggling with joy.

"Let me read you Mr. Percival's letter, just received," said Frank. "That will confirm my statement."

The whole family listened eagerly, while our hero read the letter already referred to. Of course this removed all doubt.

Mr. Hamlin was much moved.

He grasped Frank's hand, and said, fervently:

"I feel that I owe all this good fortune to you, my dear young friend. You will be able to feel that you have given me a new life, and made a whole family happy."

"I am glad on your account," said Frank; "but I must say, candidly, that if I had not believed you to be thoroughly competent, I would not have recommended you for this post."

"But would not Mr. Percival have given it to you? Have you not sacrificed your own interest to mine?"

Frank shook his head.

"I am but a boy," he said—"quite too young for such duties. Besides, I prefer to stay in New York. You are the man to discharge them to the satisfaction both of Mr. Percival and your townsmen."

Dick, who was an impulsive boy, put his arm affectionately around Frank's neck.

"Dear Frank," he said. "I liked you before; now I love you."

"I accept your friendship, Dick, and I return it fully," said Frank, warmly. "And now, Mr. Hamlin, will you accompany me to the house of Mr. Fairfield? I wish to finish my mission, and go back to New York."

"I am sorry for the poor man," said the farmer. "I suppose he doesn't deserve it, but he has my sympathy."

The two set out for the house of the agent.

CHAPTER XLIV.

THE AGENT IS NOTIFIED.

It was still early in the evening when Frank and Mr. Hamlin reached the house of the agent. Had they come five minutes later, they would have found him absent. Usually, soon after supper, he made his way to the tavern, where he spent his time and money in a very unprofitable way.

The agent was surprised when his two visitors made their appearance.

"What brings you here, Hamlin?" he asked, with scant ceremony.

"I come on a little matter of business," answered Mr. Hamlin, gravely.

Mr. Fairfield concluded that the farmer had come to make an appeal to have his rent continued at the old rates, and answered, impatiently:

"I don't think it will be of much use. My mind is made up. Have you come on business, also?" he asked, turning to Frank, with a sneer.

"Yes, sir," answered our young hero, quietly.

"That will be of no use, either," said the agent. "I am not in want of stationery, and, if I were, I should not buy of a peddler."

"I have not come here to sell stationery, Mr. Fairfield," said Frank.

"Then, may I take the liberty of asking what is your business here?"

"I come on the same business as Mr. Hamlin," answered Frank, who preferred that his companion should introduce the subject.

"Look here, I have no time for trifling," said Mr. Fairfield, angrily. "I am going out and can only spare you five minutes."

"Mr. Fairfield, I would advise you not to go out till you have heard what I have to say," said the farmer, in a meaning tone.

"I certainly shall. You can call some other time."

"Another time will not do."

"Look here, sir! Do you know to whom you are talking? How dare you use such a tone to Mr. Percival's representative?"

"I suppose you don't always expect to be Mr. Percival's representative?"

"I suppose I shall die sometime, if that's what you mean; but I am not dead yet, as you will find. To pay you for your impertinence, I shall increase your rent more than I intended. I'll drive you out of town—that's what I'll do."

This was accompanied by an angry stamp of the foot, which, however, did not frighten Mr. Hamlin much.

"I shall not pay a dollar more rent, nor shall I leave the farm I occupy," returned Mr. Hamlin, whose patience was exhausted by the rough insolence of the man before him.

"So you defy me, do you?" demanded Fairfield, furiously.

"I shall resist your injustice, sir, or rather I would do so if you were able to carry out your threat. Luckily you have not the power."

"Have not the power? You will see if I have not the power!" roared the angry agent. "I give you notice that at the end of the quarter you must go, at any rate. After your insolence, I won't let you stay on any terms. I wouldn't let you stay if you would pay double the rent. Do you hear me, Hamlin?"

"Yes, I heard you."

Mr. Fairfield looked at the farmer in surprise. The latter seemed perfectly calm and undisturbed by his threat, though it was of the most serious nature. He had expected to see him humbled, and to hear him entreat a reversal of the sentence; but his tenant was thoroughly self-possessed, and appeared to care nothing for the agent's threats.

"You need not expect that I will change my mind," he added. "Out of Jackson you must go. I know there is no other farm which you can hire, and while I am Mr. Percival's agent, you need expect no favors from me."

"I don't expect any while you are Mr. Percival's agent," said Mr. Hamlin.

There was something in the farmer's tone that arrested the agent's attention and excited his curiosity, though it did not awaken his alarm, and he could not help saying:

"Then what do you expect? Do you think I am going to die?"

"I don't expect that you will die or resign, Mr. Fairfield. You may be removed."

"Have you been writing to Mr. Percival?" exclaimed Fairfield, in mingled anger and apprehension.

"No, sir; I have not communicated with him in any way. You would not give me his address."

"Of course I would not," said the agent, feeling relieved. "It would be mere impertinence for you to write to him."

"Fortunately there is no immediate occasion for me to do so, as he has sent a representative here to investigate your official conduct."

"A representative!" exclaimed Fairfield, now thoroughly startled. "Where is he? I have not seen him."

"He is present," said Mr. Hamlin, indicating Frank.

The agent broke into a scornful laugh.

"What! the peddler?" he exclaimed. "You are either crazy, or think I am a fool."

"Neither, sir," said Frank, thinking it was time to speak. "What Mr. Hamlin says is perfectly true."

"Do you mean to tell me," said the agent, incredulously, "that Mr. Percival would send out a boy—a mere baby—to look after his affairs, and sit in judgment upon me?"

"Perhaps Mr. Percival had too much confidence in me," returned Frank, "but it is so."

"You? Why, you are a peddler!"

"Only in appearance, Mr. Fairfield. I assumed that business in order not to attract attention or excite suspicion. I am really Mr. Percival's private secretary, as I can prove to your satisfaction."

The agent regarded our hero with amazement and alarm.

"Is this true?" he asked, in a changed voice.

"Yes, sir; quite true."

"Have you written to Mr. Percival?"

"Yes, sir; and this afternoon I received a letter from him."

"What did he write?" asked Fairfield, in a husky voice; for he was convinced now that Frank spoke the truth.

"He removes you, inclosing a check for three hundred dollars in place of notice, and appoints Mr. Hamlin in your place."

"This is a hoax! You are playing a joke upon me," said Fairfield, in dismay.

"Will you read this letter, sir?"

The agent took it mechanically and read it. Badly as he had mismanaged his office, Frank could not help pitying him.

"I should like a few words with you alone," he said.

Frank followed him into an adjoining room.

"Young man," said the agent, "I want you to use your influence with Mr. Percival to keep me in office. I may have made some mistakes, but I will reform. I won't raise Hamlin's rent. In fact, I will lower it to the figure he paid in old Sampson's time. As for you, I will make it worth your while."

Frank understood very well that a bribe was meant, and answered, gravely:

"It is impossible, Mr. Fairfield."

"Then I will resist," said the agent, desperately. "What are you going to do about it?"

"You will forfeit the check I am authorized to offer you, and Mr. Percival will prosecute you for keeping back money that belongs to him."

It was enough. Fairfield knew that his management would not stand investigation, and he yielded with a bad grace.

Mr. Hamlin, the next day, to the great joy of the villagers, made known his appointment.

Fairfield left town and drifted to California, where he became an adventurer, living in a miserable and precarious manner. Mr. Hamlin moved into his fine house, and Dick was sent to a classical school to prepare for college.

The next day Frank started on his return to New York.

CHAPTER XLV.

AN IMPORTANT DISCOVERY.

ON his return to New York, Frank had no reason to be dissatisfied with his reception. From Mr. Percival to Freddie, all the family seemed delighted to see him.

"You mustn't go away again, Frank," said little Freddie. "I want to see you ever so much."

"And I wanted to see you, Freddie," said our hero, his heart warming to the little boy.

"You won't go away again, will you, Frank?"

"Not if I can help it, Freddie."

"We are all glad to see you back, Frank," said his employer. "But you have justified my opinion of you by your success. Some of my friends ridiculed me for sending a boy on such an important mission, but I don t believe any of them would have succeeded any better than you, if as well."

"I am glad you are satisfied with me, sir," said Frank, very much gratified by the commendation of his employer.

"I feel that you have done a great service, and indeed I don't know whom I could have sent in your place. However, I am glad to see you back again. I have missed you about my letters, and have postponed answering some till my young secretary returned."

Frank resumed his regular employment, and three months passed without anything that needs to be recorded.

At the end of that time, Frank received an important letter from Col. Vincent, which gave him much food for thought.

The letter was as follows:

"DEAR FRANK: For some time past I have been intending to write to you, but have delayed for no good reason. Now, however, I am led to write by a surprising discovery which has just been made in your old home, which may be of material importance to you.

"When your stepfather went away, he requested me to have an eye to the estate, and order whatever I might think necessary to be done. I am not, as you know, a very cordial friend of Mr. Manning's, but I have always regarded the property as of right belonging to you—that is, since your mother's death—and so accepted the commission.

"A few days since I went over the house and found that it was quite dirty. Where the dirt could come from in an unoccupied house I can't tell, but, at all events, I felt justified in engaging a woman to clean the paint, so, if any of you should return unexpectedly, you would find the house fit to receive you. This was a very simple matter, you will think, and scarcely needs mentioning. But, my dear Frank, events of importance often hinge on trifles, and so it has proved in the present instance.

"On the evening of the second day I received a call from Mrs. Noonan, whom I had employed to scrub the house. She had in her hand a folded paper, which she gave to me.

"'Here is something I found, sir, while I was scrubbing,' she said.

"I opened it indifferently, but conceive of my amazement when I found it to be your mother's will, properly signed, sealed and witnessed.

"Of course it was not the will which Mr. Manning presented for probate. This will gave Mr. Manning ten thousand dollars, and the residue of the property to you, except a small amount bestowed upon Richard Green, the coachman, and Deborah—sums larger, by the way, than those mentioned in the will which was read after your mother's death.

"'Where did you find this, Mrs. Noonan?' I asked.

"'Shure, sir, I was scrubbing the paint, whin, all at once, there was a little door opened in the wall, and, inside a cupboard like, I saw this paper. I thought it might be something you ought to see, and so I brought it to you, sir.'

"'And you did quite right, too, my good woman,' I replied. 'You must allow me to give you this,' and I placed a five-dollar bill in her hand.

"I was immediately showered with blessings by the grateful woman, who felt at that moment, I dare say, as rich as Crœsus, though I doubt whether she ever heard of that gentleman.

"If you were here, you would probably ask me what inference I draw from this discovery. I will not wait till I see you, but answer the question at once.

"I firmly believe, then, that the will which has just been discovered was the only will which your mother made—that Mr. Manning knew of its existence, and, being dissatisfied with it, suppressed it by hiding it where it was found. It would have been safer for him to destroy it. but that requires courage and boldness, and these are qualities which Mr. Manning does not possess.

"As to the will which was substituted in its place, my theory is that it was prepared at the instance of your stepfather by some tool of his. We must now try to discover how, or by what means, or through whose agency, this was done.

"I think you had better come up here next Saturday, and remain two or three days. This will give us a chance to confer together upon the matter."

Thus ended Col. Vincent's letter.

Frank showed it to Mr. Percival, and readily obtained permission to take a few days' vacation.

"I hope you will get back the estate, Frank," said Mr. Percival, "though I don't know what I shall do without my secretary."

"That need not separate us, Mr. Percival," said our hero. "I have no home but this."

CHAPTER XLVI.

JONAS BARTON.

FRANK started for his old home on Saturday afternoon. He would arrive in time for supper, at the house of his father's friend. The train was well filled, and he was obliged to share his seat with a shabbily dressed young man with whom, a single glance showed him, he was not likely to sympathize.

The shabby suit did not repel him at all—he was too sensible for that; but there was a furtive look in the man's face, which seemed to indicate that he was not frank and straightforward, but had something to conceal.

Half the journey passed without a word between the two. Then his companion, glancing at Frank, opened a conversation by remarking that it was a fine day.

"Very," answered Frank, laconically.

"A pleasant day to travel."

"Yes."

"Do you go far?"

Frank mentioned his destination. His companion seemed to have his interest awakened.

"Do you know a Mr. Manning, living in your town?" he asked.

"He is my stepfather," said Frank.

"Then you are Frank Courtney?" said his new acquaintance, quickly.

"I am."

"Pardon me, but I think your mother died recently?"

"Yes."

"And the property was left chiefly to Mr. Manning?"

"Yes."

"Of course, you were surprised, and very probably disappointed?"

"Excuse me," said Frank, coldly; "but I am not in the habit of discussing my affairs with strangers."

"Quite right, but I think you will find it for your interest to discuss them with me. Not in a public car, of course; but I have something of importance to communicate. Where can I have a private interview with you?"

It at once occurred to Frank that here was an opportunity, perhaps, to solve the mystery concerning the will. This man might know nothing about it; but, on the other hand, he might know everything. It would be foolish to repulse him.

"If you have anything important to tell me. I shall be glad to hear it," he said. "I am going to the house of my friend, Col. Vincent, to pass a few days. Do you know where he lives?"

"Yes, I know."

"If you will call this evening, after supper, I shall be glad to see you."

"I will do so. I will be there at eight o'clock, sharp."

On arriving at his destination, Frank found the colonel's carriage waiting for him at the station.

Col. Vincent was inside.

"Welcome, Frank!" he said, grasping heartily the hand of our young hero. "I am delighted to see you. You are looking well, and, bless me, how you have grown!"

"Thank you, Col. Vincent. Do you expect me to return the compliment?"

"About having grown? No, Frank, I hope not. I am six feet one, and don't care to grow any taller. Well, what do you think of the news?"

"I have some for you, colonel;" and Frank mentioned what his new acquaintance had told him.

"The missing link!" exclaimed the colonel, excited. "Do you know what I think?"

"What?"

"That this man either forged the will which gives the property to your stepfather, or is cognizant of it!"

"I thought of that."

"I shall be impatient to see him."

At eight o'clock the man called and gave his name as Jonas Barton. Whether it was the right name might be a question; but this did not matter.

"I understand," said Col. Vincent, "that you have some information to give us."

"I have; and that of a very important nature."

"Is it of a nature to restore to my young friend here his property, now in the possession of Mr. Manning?"

"If it were," said Jonas Barton, with a cunning glance of his left eye, "how much would it be worth?"

"I supposed it was for sale," said the colonel, quietly. "What is your own idea?"

"I will take two thousand dollars."

"Suppose we say one thousand?"

"It is not enough."

"Were you aware that the genuine will had been found?" asked the colonel, quietly.

Jonas Barton started.

"I thought Mr. Manning destroyed it," he said, hastily.

"No; he concealed it."

"Is this true?"

"Yes. You see that a part of your information has been forestalled."

"He was a fool, then, and still more a fool to refuse my last demand for money. I accept your offer of a thousand dollars, and will tell all."

"Go on."

"I wrote the will which Mr. Manning presented for probate. It was copied in part from the genuine will."

"Good! And you betray him because he will not pay what you consider the service worth?"

"Yes, sir."

Jonas Barton here gave a full account of Mr. Manning, whom he had formerly known in New York, seeking him out and proposing to him a job for which he was willing to pay five hundred dollars. Barton was not scrupulous, and readily agreed to do the work. He was skilful with the pen, and did his work so well that all were deceived.

"You will be willing to swear to this in court?"

"Yes, sir, if you will guarantee the sum you proposed."

"I will. I shall wish you to find a boarding place in the village, and remain here for the present, so as to be ready when needed. I will be responsible for your board."

As Jonas Barton was leaving the house, one

of the servants came in with important news, in which Frank was strongly interested.

CHAPTER XLVII.

CONCLUSION.

THE news was that Mr. Manning and Mark had just arrived at the Cedars. They had come by the last evening train. Why they had come back so unexpectedly no one knew, but the servant had heard that Mark was in poor health. This was true.

Mark, in Europe, had proved uncontrollable. He had given way to his natural love of drink, had kept late hours, and had seriously injured his constitution. In consequence of these excesses, he had contracted a fever, which alarmed his father and induced him to take the first steamer home.

"We won't call upon your stepfather this evening, Frank," said Col. Vincent; "but early Monday morning we will bring matters to a crisis."

Mr. Manning did not hear of Frank's presence in the village. He was fatigued with his rapid travel and kept at home. Besides, Mark was prostrated by his journey and didn't wish to be left alone.

It was, therefore, a surprise to Mr. Manning when on Monday morning, Col. Vincent was ushered into his presence, accompanied by Frank.

"Really, colonel," he said, recovering his composure, "you are very kind to call so soon. I hope you are well, Frank? Are you staying with the colonel? You must come back to your old home."

"Thank you, Mr. Manning, but I am living in New York. I am only passing a day or two with the colonel."

"It is very friendly in you to call, Col. Vincent."

"Mr. Manning," said Col. Vincent, gravely, "I am not willing to receive undeserved credit. Let me say, therefore, that this is a business, not a friendly, call."

"Indeed," said Manning, uneasily.

"The business is connected with my young friend Frank."

"I am ready to listen," said Mr. Manning. "If Frank wants a larger allowance, I am ready to give it."

"I venture to say for him that he will not be satisfied with that. Let me come to the point at once, Mr. Manning. Mrs. Manning's will has been found."

Mr. Manning started perceptibly, and his glance involuntarily wandered to that part of the wall behind which the will was discovered, for they were sitting in the very apartment where Mrs. Noonan had stumbled upon it.

"What do you mean, sir?"

"A will has been found, leaving the bulk of the property to Frank."

"Indeed! I am surprised. Is it a later will than the one which bequeathed the estate to me?" asked Mr. Manning, pointedly.

"It is Mrs. Manning's latest genuine will," said Col. Vincent, emphatically.

Mr. Manning started to his feet. He could not help understanding the colonel's meaning. It would have been idle to pretend it.

"What do you mean, Col. Vincent?" he asked, in a tone which he tried to make one of dignified resentment.

"I mean that Mrs. Manning made but one will, and that this bequeaths the property to Frank."

"How, then, do you account for the later will which was admitted to probate?"

"In this way. It was not what it purported to be."

Mr. Manning's sallow face flushed.

"What do you mean to insinuate?" he asked.

"That the last will was forged!" said Col. Vincent, bluntly.

"This is a very serious charge," said Mr. Manning, unable to repress his agitation. "You must allow me to say that I shall pay no attention to it. When you furnish proof of what you assert, it will be time enough to meet it. And now, gentlemen, if you have nothing further to say, I will bid you good-morning."

"I think you will find it best not to be in a hurry, Mr. Manning," said Col. Vincent. "The charge must be met here and now. I charge you with instigating and being cognizant of the fraud that has been perpetrated!"

"On what grounds, sir? Do you know I can sue you for libel?"

"You are welcome to do so, Mr. Manning. I have a witness who will clear me."

"Who is he?"

"Jonas Barton!"

If a bombshell had exploded in the room, Mr. Manning could not have looked paler or more thoroughly dismayed. Yet he tried to keep up a little longer.

"I don't know any man of that name," he answered, faintly.

"Your looks show that you do. I may as well tell you, Mr. Manning, that resistance is useless. We can overwhelm you with proof if we take the matter before the courts. But we do not care to do so. We have something to propose."

"What is it?" said Mr. Manning, faintly.

"The genuine will must be substituted for the fraudulent one. By it you will receive ten thousand dollars, and Frank will consent that you shall receive it. He will not ask you to account for the sums you have wrongfully spent during the last year, and will promise not to prosecute you, provided you leave this neighborhood and never return to it, or in any way interfere with him. To insure this, we shall have Jonas Barton's written confession, attested before a justice of the peace, ready for use, if needful. Do you accept?"

"I must," said Mr. Manning, despondently. "But I shall be a poor man."

"No man who has health and the use of his faculties is poor with ten thousand dollars," answered the colonel.

"Mark alone will spend more than the interest of this sum."

"Then you must prevent him. He will be better off if he has to earn his living, as Frank has done for the last year."

In less than a week the transfer was made, and Frank recovered his patrimony.

Mr. Manning and Mark went to Chicago, and perhaps further West; but nothing has been heard from them for years.

Frank didn't return to the Cedars. The place was let until he should wish to return to it.

By the advice of Col. Vincent, he resumed his preparation for college, and, graduating in due time, commenced the study of law.

Though rich enough to do without a profession, he felt that he should not be content to lead an aimless life.

He obtained for his school friend, Herbert Grant, the post of private secretary to Mr. Percival, and Herbert became nearly as great a favorite as himself.

Through Mr. Percival's kindness, Herbert was enabled, while still living at his house and attending to his duties as secretary, to enter Columbia College, and complete his course there, graduating with honor.

Herbert selected the medical profession, and, when he has completed his studies, will go abroad for a year with Frank, at the latter's expense, and, returning, open an office in New York.

While he is waiting for patients and Frank for clients, the two will live together, and their common expenses will be defrayed by Frank.

"If I didn't like you so well, Frank," said Herbert, "I would not accept this great favor at your hands——"

"But since we are dear friends," interrupts Frank, with a smile.

"I know that you enjoy giving even more than I do the receiving."

"Enough, Herbert. We understand each other. I have no brother, Herbert, and if I had, I could not care more for him than I do for you. Without you, I should feel alone in the world."

Frank does not regret the year in which he was thrown upon his own resources. It gave him strength and self-reliance; and however long he may live, he will not cease to remember with pleasure the year in which he was "Making His Way."

THE END.

POPULAR CULTURE IN AMERICA
1800-1925

An Arno Press Collection

Alger, Jr., Horatio. Making His Way; Or Frank Courtney's Struggle Upward. n. d.

Bellew, Frank. The Art of Amusing: Being a Collection of Graceful Arts, Merry Games, Odd Tricks, Curious Puzzles, and New Charades. 1866

Browne, W[illiam] Hardcastle. Witty Sayings By Witty People. 1878

Buel, J[ames] W[illiam]. The Magic City: A Massive Portfolio of Original Photographic Views of the Great World's Fair and Its Treasures of Art . . . 1894

Buntline, Ned [E. Z. C. Judson]. Buffalo Bill; And His Adventures in the West. 1886

Camp, Walter. American Football. 1891

Captivity Tales. 1974

Carter, Nicholas [John R. Coryell]. The Stolen Pay Train. n. d.

Cheever, George B. The American Common-Place Book of Poetry, With Occasional Notes. 1831

Sketches and Eccentricities of Colonel David Crockett, of West Tennessee. 1833

Evans, [Wilson], Augusta J[ane]. St. Elmo: A Novel. 1867

Finley, Martha. Elsie Dinsmore. 1896

Fitzhugh, Percy Keese. **Roy Blakeley On the Mohawk Trail.** 1925

Forester, Frank [Henry William Herbert]. **The Complete Manual For Young Sportsmen.** 1866

Frost, John. **The American Speaker:** Containing Numerous Rules, Observations, and Exercises, on Pronunciation, Pauses, Inflections, Accent and Emphasis . . . 1845

Gauvreau, Emile. **My Last Million Readers.** 1941

Haldeman-Julius, E[manuel]. **The First Hundred Million.** 1928

Johnson, Helen Kendrick. **Our Familiar Songs and Those Who Made Them.** 1909

Little Blue Books. 1974

McAlpine, Frank. **Popular Poetic Pearls,** and Biographies of Poets. 1885

McGraw, John J. **My Thirty Years in Baseball.** 1923

Old Sleuth [Harlan Halsey]. **Flyaway Ned;** Or, The Old Detective's Pupil. A Narrative of Singular Detective Adventures. 1895

Pinkerton, William A[llan]. **Train Robberies, Train Robbers, and the "Holdup" Men.** 1907

Ridpath, John Clark. **History of the United States,** Prepared Especially for Schools. Grammar School Edition, 1876

The Tribune Almanac and Political Register for 1876. 1876

Webster, Noah. **An American Selection of Lessons in Reading and Speaking.** Fifth Edition, 1789

Whiteman, Paul and Mary Margaret McBride. **Jazz.** 1926